Faithful

The Covenant God from
Eden to Eternity

JOANNA KIMBREL

STUDY SUGGESTIONS

Thank you for choosing this study to help you dig into God's Word.
We are so passionate about women getting into Scripture, and we are
praying that this study will be a tool to help you do that.

––––––––

Here are a few tips to help you get the most from this study:

- Before you begin, take time to look into the context of the book. Find out who wrote it and learn about the cultural climate it was written in, as well as where it fits on the biblical timeline. Then take time to read through the entire book of the Bible we are studying if you are able. This will help you to get the big picture of the book and will aid in comprehension, interpretation, and application.

- Start your study time with prayer. Ask God to help you understand what you are reading and allow it to transform you (Psalm 119:18).

- Look into the context of the book as well as the specific passage.

- Before reading what is written in the study, read the assigned passage. Repetitive reading is one of the best ways to study God's Word. Read it several times, if you are able, before going on to the study. Read in several translations if you find it helpful.

- As you read the text, mark down observations and questions. Write down things that stand out to you, things that you notice, or things that you don't understand. Look up important words in a dictionary or interlinear Bible.

- Look for things like verbs, commands, and references to God. Notice key terms and themes throughout the passage.

- After you have worked through the text, read what is written in the study. Take time to look up any cross-references mentioned as you study.

- Then work through the questions provided in the book. Read and answer them prayerfully.

- Paraphrase or summarize the passage, or even just one verse from the passage. Putting it into your own words helps you to slow down and think through every word.

- Focus your heart on the character of God that you have seen in this passage. What do you learn about God from the passage you have studied? Adore Him and praise Him for who He is.

- Think and pray through application and how this passage should change you. Get specific with yourself. Resist the urge to apply the passage to others. Do you have sin to confess? How should this passage impact your attitude toward people or circumstances? Does the passage command you to do something? Do you need to trust Him for something in your life? How does the truth of the gospel impact your everyday life?

- We recommend you have a Bible, pen, highlighters, and journal as you work through this study. We recommend that ballpoint pens instead of gel pens be used in the study book to prevent smearing.

Here are several other optional resources that you may find helpful as you study:

WWW.BLUELETTERBIBLE.ORG

This free website is a great resource for digging deeper. You can find translation comparison, an interlinear option to look at words in the original languages, Bible dictionaries, and even commentary.

A DICTIONARY

If looking up words in the Hebrew and Greek feels intimidating, look up words in English. Often times we assume we know the meaning of a word, but looking it up and seeing its definition can help us understand a passage better.

A DOUBLE-SPACED COPY OF THE TEXT

You can use a website like www.biblegateway.com to copy the text of a passage and print out a double-spaced copy to be able to mark on easily. Circle, underline, highlight, draw arrows, and mark in any way you would like to help you dig deeper and work through a passage.

For every one of God's
promises is *Yes* in Him.
Therefore, through Him
we also say *Amen* to
the glory of God.

2 Corinthians 1:20

table of contents

Covenants Chart

USE THIS CHART AS A TOOL WHILE YOU STUDY TO GAIN
A DEEPER UNDERSTANDING OF EACH COVENANT.

	REDEMPTION	WORKS	GRACE	NOAHIC
PROMISES *of the* COVENANT				
What it reveals about GOD'S CHARACTER				
How it is FULFILLED IN CHRIST				

ABRAHAMIC	MOSAIC	DAVIDIC	NEW COVENANT

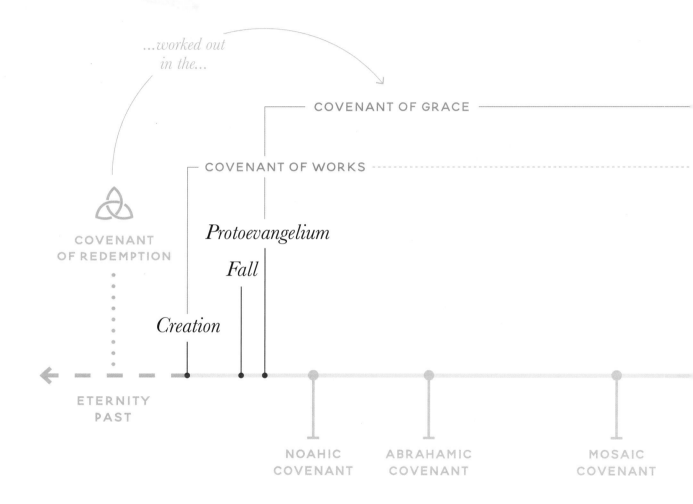

...*worked out in the...*

COVENANT OF GRACE

COVENANT OF WORKS

COVENANT
OF REDEMPTION

Protoevangelium

Fall

Creation

ETERNITY
PAST

NOAHIC
COVENANT

ABRAHAMIC
COVENANT

MOSAIC
COVENANT

Covenants Timeline

FROM THE COVENANT OF REDEMPTION FORMED IN ETERNITY PAST TO
THE CONSUMMATION OF THE NEW COVENANT AT CHRIST'S SECOND COMING

Christ's 2nd Coming

DAVIDIC COVENANT

NEW COVENANT INAUGURATED

NEW COVENANT CONSUMMATED

ETERNITY FUTURE

Signs of the Covenants

NOAHIC COVENANT

— *Rainbow* —

ABRAHAMIC COVENANT

— *Circumcision* —

MOSAIC COVENANT

— *Sabbath* —

DAVIDIC COVENANT

— *Throne* —

NEW COVENANT

— *Baptism* —

The God Who Works in History

Read Romans 16:25-27, Hebrews 1:1-4, 1 Peter 1:10-12

The Lord is a God who makes Himself known.

From the garden of Eden all the way to eternity, God is graciously revealing Himself to mankind. The eternal God of the universe who exists outside of time chooses to reveal Himself to the world through history.

God has been declaring who He is from the beginning, ever since He breathed life into Adam. This revelation is progressive—truth building on truth—unfolding in God's perfect and sovereign timing to bring about the fulfillment of every promise through Christ in "the fullness of time" (Galatians 4:4). His Word, the Bible, communicates the gradual unveiling of His character in the story of redemption, and this grand narrative finds its framework in covenants.

Flipping between the Old Testament and the New Testament without any sense of how it all fits together can cause confusion. It might seem as if they are two different stories that are nearly impossible to reconcile, and that the God of the Old Testament is entirely different from the God of the New Testament. However, the Old Testament is not contradictory to the New Testament; it is simply incomplete. As the story of Scripture unfolds, it does not contradict itself but progressively reveals God's character and His plan of redemption.

Every bit of the Bible is about Jesus, and God works in every covenant that He establishes in Scripture to point to the One who fulfills them all. Approaching Scripture with the understanding that all of it is perfectly united in Christ, that every book is pointing to Jesus, and that every verse is about Him, can help to shed light on the meaning of even the most difficult passages.

Believers today have the incredible blessing of living after the first coming of Jesus Christ and reading the eye-witness accounts of His life, death, and resurrection from those who knew Him and were called to be His apostles. The New Testament reveals how promises and prophecies are miraculously fulfilled in Christ, but those whom God used to pen those prophecies did not have that same luxury. As the author of Hebrews explains, God has spoken to His people in a variety of ways and times throughout history, and before Christ, He spoke by revealing Himself and His plan of redemption through prophets. These prophecies did not give a full and clear picture of what was to come, but these veiled promises are uncovered in the person of Jesus Christ. He is the One who radiates God's glory. He is the One who makes the Father known (John 1:18). The prophets and fathers who came before Christ did not see the full picture. They searched and inquired, longing to know how these prophecies would be fulfilled, searching for the One who would be the yes to every promise. Even the angels longed to look into the fullness of the gospel in Jesus

Christ. In God's partial revelation they did not see how all that was promised would come to pass, but they believed that "He who promised is faithful" (Hebrews 10:23).

Contemporary Christians have the opportunity to see clearly so much more than those whose stories appear in the Old Testament, but God's progressive revelation has not yet come to an end. As God's self-revelation has progressed, His plan to work in history has been further illuminated, but there is still much that is yet to be revealed. The world has seen many promises fulfilled, but there are still more prophecies that have yet to come to fruition. God's people wait eagerly for the day when the suffering of this life will be no more. Those who are in Christ can hope in expectation for the hour when Christ will return to make all things new—when sin and death will be no more, when the tireless battle against sin will be brought to an end, and when all will be right.

Meanwhile, the entire world is broken, none of it untouched by the curse of the fall. God promises to work all things together for the good of those who love Him, but in the midst of suffering, it can be difficult or even impossible to see how that could be true. God promises a day when the pain will be no more, but in the meantime, living in a sin-cursed world makes it difficult to understand the purpose of enduring struggles and trials. The "hows" and "whys" may not be apparent, but knowing the "who" is enough. When the circumstances of life are marked by pain or tragedy that seems senseless and the full picture of how God is working is not clear, this truth remains: understanding the full story is not required to trust the God who is writing it. As circumstances change, there is rest in the character of the unchanging God. He is good, He is sovereign, and He is kind.

Moment by moment, year by year, covenant by covenant, God is revealing Himself and His plan to redeem a people for His own possession. In His great mercy, He invites us to come and see. To taste of His goodness. To marvel at His grace. To be enraptured by His loving-kindness. To delight in His story and rejoice in the truth that in Christ it is our story too. As we embark on this journey through God's Word, we will trace the unfolding story of our covenant-making, covenant-keeping God.

What do today's Scripture passages reveal about how God works in history?

....

....

....

....

....

Do you ever have a hard time understanding how the Old Testament and the New Testament fit together? What is one thing in the Old Testament that you struggle to reconcile with the New Testament?

....

....

....

....

....

....

In what areas of your life do you struggle with the unknown? How can you rest in God's character in that circumstance?

....

....

....

....

....

....

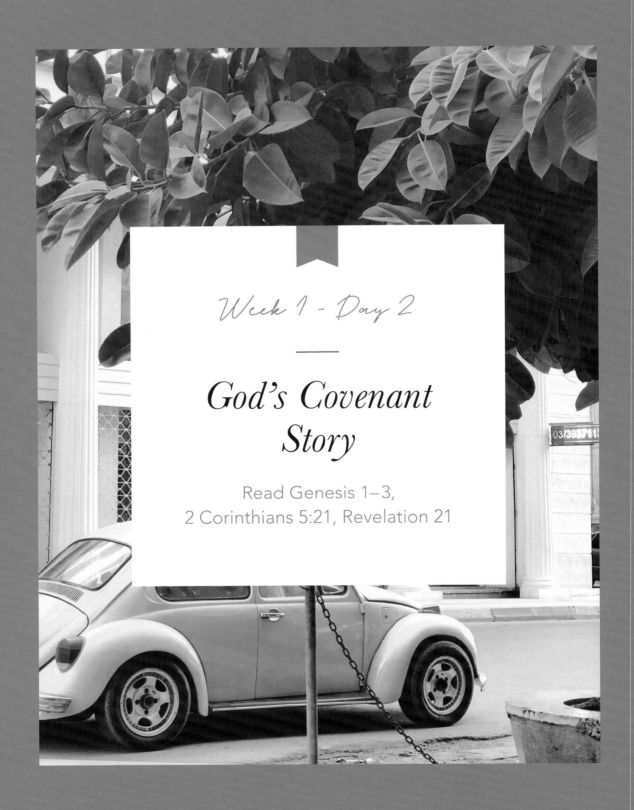

Week 1 - Day 2

—

God's Covenant Story

Read Genesis 1–3,
2 Corinthians 5:21, Revelation 21

Even before Jesus took on human form, God's Word was pointing to Him.

The entire Bible tells one story of a covenant-making, covenant-keeping God and His plan to redeem His people. God saves through covenants, and in order to understand how all of the covenants of Scripture function together, we must first understand the metanarrative of Scripture, which is the larger, overarching story of redemption that spans the entire Bible. As God's self-revelation through covenants progresses, Scripture shows the unfolding of the story of redemption that God is writing in four plot movements. The four categories that reflect different parts of the story of redemption are Creation, Fall, Redemption, and Consummation.

Creation. The first book of the Bible, Genesis, reveals that everything originated from the only uncreated being, God Himself. He created the universe and He called it good. He created man in His own image, entering into a covenant relationship with them and calling them to be His ambassadors on earth. God dwelt among His people; He walked with them and communed with them. Not only did man not experience evil, but he also had no knowledge of it. He had no condemning shame, no whispers of anxiety, no fear of loss. All was well.

Fall. In Genesis 3, Adam and Eve break covenant. They disobey God, and sin enters the world. The consequences of sin are devastating and far-reaching. Mankind, once pure and in the continual presence of the holy God, are now unclean and consumed by shame, and God sends them away from His presence. Sin always results in death, and it does not take long after the fall to see that the world is indeed dying. The effects of sin do not stop with Adam and Eve, but are passed on to every generation. Within one generation, the sinful nature of man is put on horrific display as Cain murders his brother Abel out of jealousy. By Genesis 6, humanity has declined to the point that their wicked hearts are described as inclined only toward evil at all times. It is easy to see the effects of sin in the world today. Whether it be poverty or natural disasters, disease or hatred, tragedy or shame, there is no denying the devastation of the fall.

Redemption. God does not leave us in our hopelessness. From the very beginning, God has been working to save His people. Even as he pronounces the curse of sin in Eden, God establishes another covenant with Adam and Eve—a covenant not based on works, but on grace—a covenant that promises the redemption of God's people in spite of their sin. Jesus Christ accomplishes the work of redemption, saving us from our own sin, a task that we could never do on our own. Our promised Messiah, the One whom God promised from the very beginning, gave His own life to pay our penalty of death for our sins so that we might take on His righteousness and appear holy and blameless before the

almighty God. Even before Jesus took on human form, God's Word was pointing to Him. God uses flawed people throughout history to foreshadow and reflect the better redeemer to come. Every covenant finds its fulfillment in Him.

Consummation or Restoration. God not only saves us from His wrath against sin, but He blesses us beyond anything we could ever think or imagine. Even after we have been justified by God's amazing grace, it is clear that we still live in a broken and fallen world. We still wrestle with the sinfulness of our hearts, and we are reminded daily that things are not as they should be. Our God is a God who restores above and beyond what was lost, even though our own sin is the reason for the brokenness. God's covenant promises find their completion in the good news that Christ will return, and when He does, He will make all things new. Revelation 21 describes the consummation of Christ's kingdom in the new heaven and new earth, a place where sin and death and sadness are no more, and where God dwells with His people, a people made pure and holy by the blood of Christ.

The story of Scripture is connected by a series of covenants established by God for the purpose of revealing Himself and redeeming His people. When we see the stories of the Bible in light of the bigger story, they take on new meaning and reveal to us more fully the beautiful character of our righteous God — the God who keeps covenant with His people.

The entire Bible tells one story of a covenant-making, covenant-keeping God and His plan to redeem His people.

Have you ever considered the Bible as one big story?
Why is it important to read the Bible this way?

....
....
....
....
....

In your own words, briefly summarize the overarching story of the Bible.

....
....
....
....
....
....
....
....

How do you see the metanarrative of Scripture reflected in your own life?
How have you seen God's redemption in the midst of your own brokenness?

....
....
....
....
....
....
....

God's Covenant Faithfulness

Read Psalm 136, Romans 8:31-39

A covenant is a promise, and God always comes through on His promises.

God is relational. God is a covenant-making God, and he has related to humans by covenants throughout all of history. We cannot have a complete understanding of our relationship to Him apart from an understanding of these covenants. The story of Scripture is saturated with the language of covenants, with the Hebrew and Greek words *berit* and *diatheke* appearing more than 300 times in the Bible. Covenants are an integral part of God's work in history and they provide a framework for understanding Scripture. Covenants matter, but what exactly is a covenant?

Strictly defining a covenant is a difficult task since the elements can vary based on the situation. At its most basic level, a covenant is an agreement between two or more parties. Covenants are legally binding. They frequently have terms that each party must uphold, and the adherence to those terms often brings consequences: blessings for obedience and curses for disobedience. A covenant often has some kind of sign to indicate that it has been established.

This description might make a covenant seem synonymous with a contract, but covenants are so much more than that. Unlike a contract with an internet provider or the company that remodels a kitchen, covenants are deeply personal. A covenant is much more like a marriage than a business partnership. To enter into covenant is to enter into a binding relationship with someone—a relationship that is not just business, but is profoundly intimate. Covenants connect its members to one another, powerfully binding them together. Every covenant covered in this study is a covenant established by God—the eternal, infinite, all-powerful God of the universe—choosing to enter into an intimate relationship with sinful people.

A covenant is a promise, and God always comes through on His promises. God is a covenant-making, covenant-keeping God. Scripture frequently uses the Hebrew word *hesed* to describe God's character, a word that embodies His covenant-faithfulness. *Hesed* describes God's mercy to sinners in offering them redemption. It proclaims His loving-kindness to save those who have made themselves enemies of God from His wrath and adopt them as His own children. *Hesed* is a loyal, enduring, steadfast love that never gives up, never abandons, and never backs out on a promise. It is the goodness of God that works in every single second of history to bring about the redemption that He promises to His people. *Hesed* is covenant love. It is a love that stays even when it is not reciprocated.

The pages of Scripture testify to the loyal, covenant love of God. This *hesed* is a love that works on behalf of God's people. In Psalm 136, David recounts the deeds of the

Lord who acts in steadfast love—in *hesed*—from creation all the way to eternity. In the first three verses, David calls on God's people to give Him thanks for His goodness and steadfast love, and His *hesed* is certainly a reason to rejoice! Knowing that the perfect and holy God of the universe chooses to show unrelenting love to sinners should be cause for unceasing praise. David then harkens back to the creation account in Genesis, bringing to mind God's enduring love that is faithful in creating and sustaining the universe and its inhabitants with whom He would establish His covenant. David recounts the works of God who delivered His covenant people, the Israelites, from their slavery in Egypt, just as He delivers all believers, His covenant people, from slavery to sin. Even as they wandered in the wilderness, grumbling, complaining and turning to worship idols, God's steadfast love remained and He kept covenant with His people. In His mercy, God delivered them from kings and rulers who sought to overtake them. In His covenant faithfulness, He brought them into the land He promised them, just as He will bring His people at last to a new heaven and new earth. The *hesed* of God—his mercy, goodness, and kindness to keep His covenant to His people—will not fade away. It endures forever.

God is faithful to fulfill His covenants, and He fulfills every one in Christ. Jesus is the yes to every promise from God (2 Corinthians 1:20). Even before He formed the foundations of the world, God made a plan to enter into covenant with sinners who would be made righteous by the blood of Christ. In Christ, the enemy is defeated. In Christ, God's wrath is satisfied. In Christ, the righteous requirement of the law is fulfilled. In Christ, the promise of blessing is made a reality. In Christ, the hope of an eternal King comes true. In Christ, all will be made right and new in the presence of God.

If you are in Christ, rest in this good news: the covenant-faithfulness of God is on your side, and nothing can separate you from His love. God is committed to you because He has entered into covenant with you. You are His. What then should we fear? What can overtake us? What could come against us? If God is for us, there is not anything that can defeat us. Our unchanging God has proven Himself to be faithful time and time again, and He will be faithful to you.

*In Psalm 136, David uses the word hesed to talk about God's character.
Depending on the version of the Bible you are using, it may be translated as love,
steadfast love, mercy, or lovingkindness. How many times does the word hesed
appear in Psalm 136, and what does it reveal about God's character?*

....
....
....
....
....

How does God's steadfast love toward us differ from how we tend to respond to Him?

....
....
....
....
....
....

How have you seen God's hesed in your own life?

....
....
....
....
....
....
....
....
....

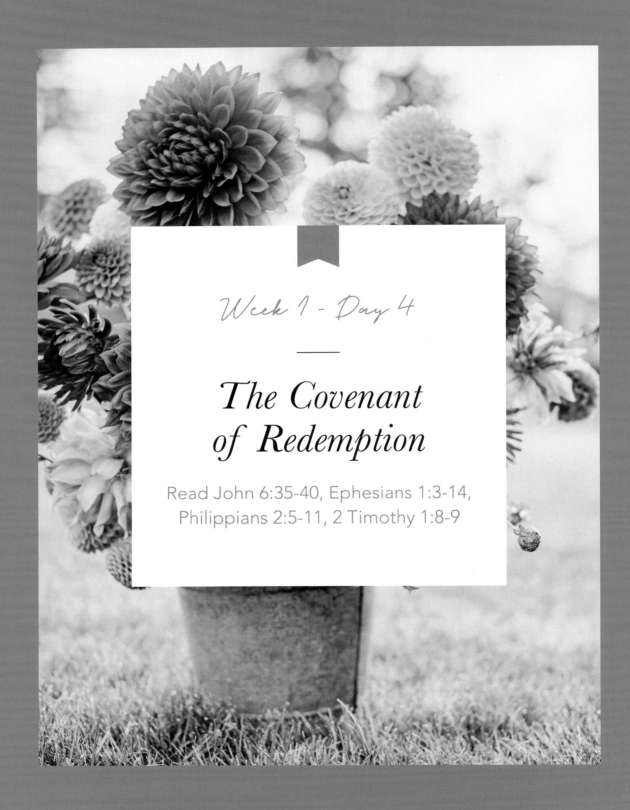

Week 1 - Day 4

The Covenant of Redemption

Read John 6:35-40, Ephesians 1:3-14,
Philippians 2:5-11, 2 Timothy 1:8-9

Before time began,
God entered into a covenant.

Before the world was formed, before He breathed life into Adam, and before the world was cursed from sin, God covenanted to save a people for Himself. The unchanging God has always been merciful, even before there was a need for mercy. The immutable God has always been abounding in *hesed* — His covenant faithfulness and steadfast love — even before He spoke the first word of creation. Before there was a need for grace and forgiveness, God met it by entering into the covenant of redemption.

The members of the Trinity formed the covenant of redemption before God created the universe and before time began, in which the Son agreed to redeem those whom the Father had chosen. It is a pre-temporal, intratrinitarian covenant. It is by virtue of this covenant and its outworkings that believers can have eternal life in Christ. Through this covenant, God's eternal plan of redemption comes to pass. In this covenant, the Son agreed to become a man, Jesus Christ, and to live on earth in perfect obedience and righteousness. He covenanted to submit to the will of the Father in order to save His elect through His obedience even to the point of dying on the cross to pay sin's penalty of death in their place. As a blessing for upholding the covenant, the Father promised to give the Son a pure and spotless bride. This bride is the Church, which is made up of all believers whom God purifies for the day when Christ will return once again. Because of His obedience, the Father exalts the Son and bestows on Him glory and honor at the right hand of the Father.

God not only planned the redemption of His people, but He also chose those whom He would redeem. God elected a people for Himself in Christ before He ever laid the foundations of the world. He set them apart to be forgiven, holy, and lavished with the blessings of His grace. He chose them to be adopted as His children, and what God has ordained by His will He always brings to pass. The covenant commitment God made to His own was a bond made from the beginning, and that covenant cannot be broken. The redemption of God's people is secure.

The unfolding of this covenant takes place throughout the entire course of history, without a single moment occurring outside of God's plan. The story of Scripture is the account of God working in time to fulfill this one foundational covenant. God is working in the covenant of redemption and every covenant thereafter to redeem His people, and all of God's covenants find their fulfillment in Christ. Jesus is the yes to all the promises of God (2 Corinthians 1:20). Jesus is the complete fulfillment of each covenant God establishes. Christ is on every page and in every promise from Genesis to Revelation.

From eternity past, Jesus Christ was the plan to save lost sinners, and not a single moment is outside of God's sovereign will to make it so. If you are in Christ, that means that every failure and victory, every bit of heartbreak and rejoicing, every pain and comfort — God is using all of it to purify you and make you holy for the day of Christ's return to be presented to Him as His bride. When the chaos of this world and the unexplainable suffering seems senseless, the covenant of redemption declares that all of it has a purpose. It is not meaningless.

In the front of this book, there is a chart for you to fill out as you work through the covenants. This chart will help you to reflect on the covenants, how they reveal God's character, and how they are fulfilled in Christ. Add to your chart as you study so that you can look back and see a big picture view of how God is working in history to redeem His people. As we journey through our study, may we direct our gaze to Christ who completes them all.

What God has ordained by His will
He always brings to pass.

Reread Ephesians 1:3-14 and write down a list of the things that God does for those who are in Christ. How does this passage enhance your understanding of how the covenant of redemption impacts your salvation?

....
....
....
....
....
....
....

How does the covenant of redemption reassure you when you make mistakes and fall into sin?

....
....
....
....
....
....
....

What does the covenant of redemption reveal about God's character?

....
....
....
....
....
....
....

Creation and
The Covenant of Works

Read Genesis 1–2

To live is grace upon grace, and every good thing that we experience is a gift.

In the beginning, God created. From nothing, He created the heavens and the earth, water and dry land, the sun and moon and stars, day and night and seasons, animals and fish and birds. In His crowning act of all creation, God made human beings in His own image to reflect His character.

When God creates Adam and Eve in Eden, He establishes a covenant with them called the covenant of works. Although the Genesis account does not include the word covenant, all of the elements of a covenant are present. It has terms to be upheld with blessings for obedience and curses for disobedience. It legally binds God and mankind in a relationship together.

When God establishes the covenant of works with Adam and Eve, he lays out the terms they must uphold. The covenant requires perfect obedience to God—perfect good works. On the one hand, obedience means fulfilling the command God gives to Adam and Eve in the garden to live as the *imago dei*, the image of God. As God's image bearers they are called to carry out the work of God on the earth. Just as God created the earth and filled it, Adam and Eve are to reflect His character through procreation and fill the earth with more image bearers. They are to work the earth, subduing it and bringing order. Adam and Eve are God's co-regents on earth, ruling as His representatives, working as He works, resting as He rests. All of these things are part of what theologians call the cultural mandate that God gives to the first humans. Perfect obedience means not only fulfilling this God-given mandate, but also observing the one prohibition that God gives them: they must not eat the fruit of the Tree of the Knowledge of Good and Evil. The prohibition is the central element of the covenant. To break it would bring a covenant curse, and to perfectly obey the terms of the covenant would bring a covenant blessing.

The curse of the covenant of works, should it be broken, is death—the consequence of sin that God clearly lays out in Genesis 2:17. Those who knew nothing but life and joy and peace in God's presence would face pain and destruction. They would taste death in a world that previously had tasted none of it. The consequences of sin would be devastating.

But why do Adam and Eve need perfect obedience? Why are the standards so high? God requires perfect obedience because God is perfectly holy. God has no flaws or shortcomings. God never sins. He never makes mistakes. He never does anything that is not perfectly good. God is infinite in purity, in righteousness, and in goodness. God is holy, and when His image bearers make even the smallest mistake, it mars the image of the all-holy God in them. Even the smallest act of rebellion is a serious offense against Him.

His holiness is also the reason for the curse. God's holiness necessitates His justice. God does what is right, and all sin—any disobedience—must be punished in order for God's justice to stand. If God did not punish sin, He would not be just. If God were not just, He would not be holy. If God were not holy, He would not be God.

The covenant of works also includes implied blessings for obedience. The natural outcomes of obedience in themselves would be blessings to Adam and Eve, like the joy of children and the fruits of their labor, but the blessing does not end there. God would bless them abundantly more. Instead of death and pain and toilsome work, obedience would lead to unending, incorruptible life in the perfect presence of God in a world that would yield good fruit from pleasant labor. This reality would be a life without suffering; a life of complete joy and eternal pleasures in God's presence (Psalm 16:11).

Although the covenant of works is not a covenant based on redeeming grace, it is abounding with God's condescending grace, which is the grace to draw near and offer undeserved blessings. Adam and Eve are God's creations, and that fact alone necessitates their perfect obedience. All people owe obedience to God simply because He created them. The fact that God would offer any kind of blessing is not because Adam and Eve are entitled to it, but because God is rich in grace and gives good gifts to His children.

We have a tendency toward entitlement. We can grow bitter toward God, questioning why He has not given us all the blessings we desire, all the while forgetting that even the smallest good that we experience is an act of grace that would be undeserved even for a creature of God who could walk in perfect obedience, much less for sinful humans like us. To live is grace upon grace, and every good thing that we experience is a gift—not a payment for faithfulness that we already owe—from our gracious God (James 1:7). May we live not in bitterness and frustration for what we lack, but in awestruck gratitude for the God who gives far above anything we could ever think or imagine (Ephesians 3:20).

What does the covenant of works reveal about God's character?

....

....

....

....

....

....

....

*The covenant of works requires perfect obedience to all of God's commands.
Is this something you are able to uphold in your own life?*

....

....

....

....

....

....

....

*Where do you see tendencies toward entitlement in your own heart and life?
Write a prayer of confession to God and thank Him for the undeserved
blessings He has given you.*

....

....

....

....

....

....

— WEEK 1 —

Give thanks to the Lord, for he is good. His faithful love endures forever.

Psalm 136:1

— DAY 6 —

Week One *Reflection*

Answer the following questions about this week's Scripture passages.

How did the text increase your understanding of covenants?

....
....
....
....
....

What did you observe about God's character?

....
....
....
....
....

What did you learn about the condition of mankind and about yourself?

....
....
....
....
....

How does the text point to the gospel?

....
....
....
....
....
....

How should you respond to this week's text? What is the practical application?

....
....
....
....
....
....

What specific action steps can you take this week to apply the text?

....
....
....
....
....
....

Covenant-Breakers

Read Genesis 3

All of God's commands are good...but the enemy whispers a different story.

It does not take long after God establishes His covenant of works with Adam and Eve that they fail to uphold its terms. God has revealed Himself in His Word as the faithful covenant-maker and covenant-keeper, and now in Genesis 3, humankind reveals themselves to be covenant-breakers for the first time, but certainly not the last.

God lavishes Adam and Eve with undeserved blessings and lovingly gives them boundaries that would keep them safe. Not only does humanity owe obedience to their Creator, but this obedience produces the best life possible. Although Adam and Eve do not possess infinite knowledge, God gives them the knowledge that they need. They have enough to know that they can trust the One who is omniscient. Obedience does not require an understanding of the why behind God's commands because the who behind the commands is enough.

All of God's commands are good, and all of God's commands are for joy, but the enemy whispers a different story. When the devil comes sowing doubt and discontentment in the minds of Adam and Eve, they listen. They choose to believe the deception of the serpent instead of their gracious God.

They believe the lie that God is keeping something good from them.
They believe the lie that God is deceiving them.
They believe the lie that there is wisdom to be found apart from God.
They believe the lie that God is not enough to satisfy them.
They believe the lie that giving in to temptation would be worth the consequences.
They believe the lie that they need to have as much knowledge as God in order to trust Him.
They believe the lie that it is better for them to be in control than for God to be in control.
They believe the lie that God desires anything but the best for them.

Adam and Eve have the ability to obey, but they choose disobedience. They choose to follow the one who comes to steal and kill and destroy instead of the One who gives abundant life (John 10:10). They take the fruit and they eat. They transgress the covenant (Hosea 6:7) and usher in the covenant curse. The heartbreaking reality of Adam and Eve's rejection of their gracious God quickly sets in, and the effects of the curse are far-reaching. The curse would impact the physical world, with the ground producing thorns and thistles where there was once only fruitfulness. It would strain marriages and bring pain to the process of bearing and raising children. Just as God warned, the curse of sin means the beginning of death. Not only do Adam and Eve suffer spiritual death, but from the moment that they sin, their bodies begin the journey back to the dust from which they were formed as they become subject to sickness and decay. Sin produces the devastating consequences of death and separation from God.

The covenant curse extends far beyond Adam and Eve. Covenants function with federal headship, which means that a covenant representative acts on behalf of others who are bound by the same covenant. The covenant of works is not just a covenant that God makes with Adam and Eve, but a covenant that He makes with all of humanity with Adam as the covenant head. Adam, then, is the representative for every person who would ever live, so that what is true of Adam concerning the covenant is also true of every human being who comes after him. Eating the fruit in the garden does not only mark the fall of Adam and Eve, but it marks the fall of man as a whole. Because of Adam's sin, we are all born sinful. Through Adam, we have inherited sin. Through Adam, we have inherited death. Because of the fall, every single one of us is born into sin and every single one of us has a life marked by sin. We have inherited a sinful nature and our spiritual deadness predisposes us to choose the lies of the enemy over the holiness of God. While Adam was able to choose perfect obedience, we cannot. We are born not as children of God but as His enemies. We are all covenant-breakers, and in our sin, we are all condemned to death under the covenant curse.

The situation seems hopeless, and it is good for us to feel the weight of sin and our own helplessness to remedy our sin problem. We need to see our own need. The damage has been done. The sentence has been declared. Our first covenant head has failed. Therefore, we have all failed. But the Word of God pulses with the ever-present hope of redemption — sometimes in whispers and others with banners and shouts. Scripture heralds the coming of the One who would do what Adam could not: Christ, the One who would break the power of sin by becoming the curse of the covenant on our behalf. The Bible directs our gaze to Jesus on every page, from the garden to eternity.

Christ would come to fulfill the covenant, but not yet. Adam and Eve faced the consequences of a world and of bodies and hearts stained by the curse of sin, and we all live in that same reality. The effects of the fall are all around us, but we do not live like those without hope. We have hope in the better Adam. We have hope in Christ.

*A thief comes only to steal and kill and destroy. I have come
so that they may have life and have it in abundance.*

JOHN 10:10

Adam and Eve chose to believe the lies of the serpent rather than the promises of God. How do you see this tendency in your own life? What are some lies that you believe?

What consequences does Adam's sin have for us? How do you see the effects of the fall in your own heart and life and in the world around you?

How does considering the tragedy of the fall affect the way you view salvation?

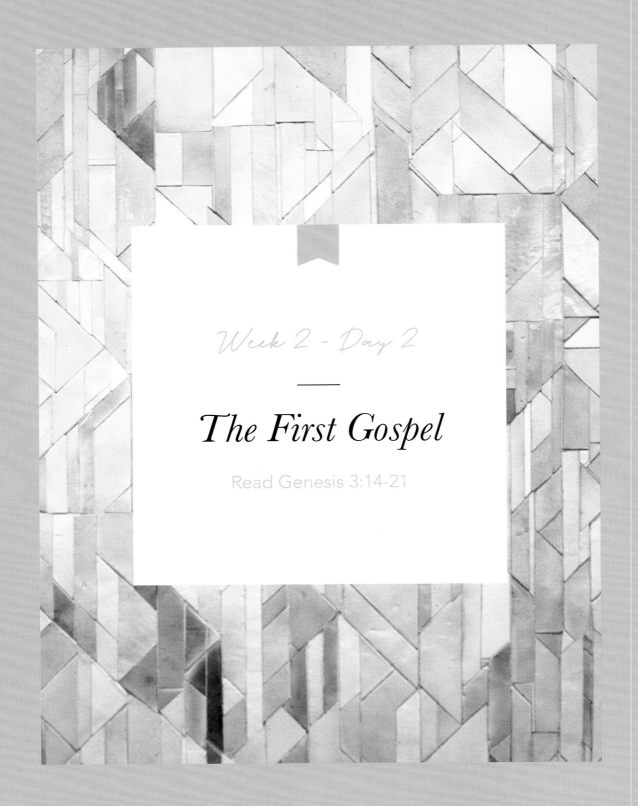

Week 2 - Day 2

The First Gospel

Read Genesis 3:14-21

When darkness entered the world,
God promised light.

We may be covenant-breakers, but God is not. Before the foundation of the world, God covenanted to redeem a people for Himself. In the midst of the heart-wrenching consequences of the fall of man, that promise may seem lost, but God always fulfills His promises, even when we do not understand how it can be so. Even as God pronounces the covenant curse, He gives unimaginable hope. From the very beginning, it is abundantly clear that God is in the business of bringing about redemption. God brings light from darkness, beauty from ashes, and joy from pain.

Genesis 3:15 is known as the protoevangelium, which means "the first gospel." The gospel is the good news of salvation for sinners, and God made the gospel known as soon as man's first sin. When darkness entered the world, God promised light. When man brought about his own brokenness, God promised healing. The gospel did not begin on Christmas day, but God planned to give Himself for sinners before the first "let there be." God announced the good news of salvation as soon as its necessity was apparent, and He works throughout all of Scripture and throughout all of history to bring about His plan of redemption.

In this first veiled promise of redemption, God reveals that a savior would come and that He would be the offspring of the woman. Through her seed, One would come who would save God's people from the death they inflicted upon themselves through sin. Through the line of the sinful woman would come One who would be without sin but who would become the curse of sin so that God's elect would not have to bear it. From the woman would come One who would give life to those who earned death. Eve would look for the Savior in her own son, but God's plan extends far beyond what she could see. The pages of the Old Testament are filled with longing and waiting for the promised offspring as the people of God see their hope delayed with each insufficient prophet, priest, and king. God would send the Redeemer, but not yet.

This first gospel reveals that the promised Savior would suffer. The serpent would wound, but he would not have victory over Christ. The suffering servant would endure the pain of the cross, but even His death would not be final. When Christ died on the cross, it seemed as if the devil had won and hope was lost, but even though Satan bruised the Savior's heel, the wounds left by the serpent would be the very thing that would crush him under the feet of Jesus. Christ is not defeated in His death, but victorious over the power of sin and death in His resurrection.

Adam and Eve moved forward into the devastating reality of a world marked by sin, but God did not leave them without hope. Adam and Eve did not know when or how the Savior would come, but they could trust in the faithful promises of God that He would. We have the privilege of seeing the protoevangelium from the perspective of this side of the cross. We can trace the faithfulness of God throughout the Old Testament and see glimpses of God's sovereign hand working in every moment of history to bring about His promises for His people. Like Adam and Eve, we can live in a broken world with confident hope because we know how the story ends. We experience the effects of sin every day as we are surrounded by brokenness and injustice. We feel the weight of death in our bodies as we suffer from illness, fatigue, and decay and we walk with the pain of broken relationships torn apart by sin. Even so, we do not live like those without hope. We can walk with joy in a sin-sick world because we know the end of the story. No matter what we endure, we can trust the God who will redeem all that was lost. We can look back to Christ's first coming, but we still hope for the day when He will come again. Like our first parents, we do not know when He will return or how God is working in every moment, but we can trust the God who is always faithful.

God brings light from darkness,
beauty from ashes, and joy from pain.

What does God's first promise of the gospel reveal about His character?

....

....

....

....

....

....

How should your understanding of the protoevangelium in Genesis 3 impact the way you study Scripture?

....

....

....

....

....

....

How does looking back to God's faithfulness to fulfill His promises and looking forward to the promise of Christ's second coming give you hope in your current circumstances?

....

....

....

....

....

....

The Covenant of Grace

Read Ephesians 2:1-9, Hebrews 11

For Adam and Eve, the covenant of works was a matter of life and death, and through their disobedience they chose death. Because Adam is our covenant head, his sin meant death not only for himself, but also for all of us. The fall of man means that no one can measure up to the perfect obedience required by the covenant of works, and all are justly condemned to the curse of the covenant, which is death.

Hope may seem lost, but on the day that man falls, God initiates a covenant founded not on works, but on grace. From Genesis 3 on, all those who are in Christ are no longer under the covenant of works, but under the covenant of grace, because Christ has fulfilled the covenant of works on our behalf.

The covenant of grace is the outworking of the covenant of redemption that God established in eternity past. Through the covenant of grace, God relates to His people with a sacrificial, undeserved, merciful love. It is through this covenant that God reconciles sinners to Himself, saves them from the curse of death, and gives them eternal life with Him. Because of the covenant of grace, sinners can be saved not by good works, as every person would fall terribly short, but by the abundant grace of God through faith in the work of Christ.

The grace of God is God's unmerited favor. Although God's undeserved blessings for humanity existed before the fall, it is only when sin enters the world that God's saving grace becomes necessary and active. Adam and Eve transgressed the covenant, and the covenant curse of death was rightly theirs, but God in His amazing love establishes another covenant, a covenant that would not depend on man, but on God. The perfectly holy and righteous God of the universe chooses to obligate Himself to sinful humans who made themselves His enemies.

While the terms of the covenant of works required perfect obedience from man, the terms of the covenant of grace for man only require faith. The faith that is required is believing God for the promise of a savior given as early as Genesis 3:15. It is entrusting our very lives to Him, knowing full well that it is impossible for us to fulfill the covenant of works in our fallen state. It is understanding that the only way we could ever escape the covenant curse and partake in covenant blessings is by the grace of God and trusting in that grace to save us. The rest of the covenant terms fall completely on God. He obligates Himself to man to save him, to purify him, to glorify him with Christ, and to give him eternal life in God's presence. The weight of the covenant of grace falls not on man, but on God. Even the faith that is required of us is a gift from God, the One who establishes and sustains our faith (Hebrews 12:2). We are saved by grace through faith.

Because the covenant is dependent on God and not on us, we can have complete assurance that if God has established His covenant of grace with us, evidenced by the faith He gives, we are fully secure in His promises. If the blessings of the covenant depended on us, we would spend our lives in constant striving to earn His favor and we would most certainly fail, but God always fulfills His promises. God never forgets His covenant. He has established an unbreakable bond with us that He will never abandon. We are safe in His love, not because of our faithfulness, but because of His.

From the moment that God announces the covenant of grace in Genesis 3:15, all future covenants that He establishes with man are administrations of this one, overarching covenant of grace that progressively reveals God's plan of redemption for His people. Throughout all of history, every person who finds salvation finds it under the covenant of grace. Every one of God's people receives salvation in the same way — by grace through faith in Jesus Christ. Hebrews lists person after person from the Old Testament, from Abel to Rahab and beyond, who received their approval not by their works, but by faith. But how could faith in Jesus Christ be the source of salvation for those who lived before He came to the earth as a man? How could they have faith in a person whom they had not yet known or seen? They had faith because they were assured of what they hoped for — they believed in the promises of God to send a savior. They had faith because they believed with conviction what they could not see — the life, death, and resurrection of Jesus Christ on their behalf. Christ's blood did not just cover the sins of his contemporary and future followers, but God in His eternal plan to save sinners through the death of His son forgave the sins of those who put their faith in the future promise of the Redeemer (Romans 3:25).

The promise of salvation, though veiled at first, is for all of His people throughout all of history by the same means — by grace through faith. As the story of Scripture unfolds, our blurred understanding of God's administration of the covenant of grace comes into focus as the veil is torn and God's way of grace is revealed — that Christ died for our sins. As we look to Christ, we can look back on the pages of Scripture and see more clearly how God was working out His plan of redemption through the covenant of grace, every bit of which points to Jesus Christ. Even now our vision of grace is obstructed by temporary things, but we hope in the day when we will see God face to face and see His glorious grace for all that it is (1 Corinthians 12:12). Like those who have come before us, we hope in the homeland that we long for and see from afar, a homeland where we will enjoy the unmerited blessings of the covenant of grace as we will dwell with God.

The weight of the covenant of grace falls
not on man, but on God.

Ephesians 2:1-9 gives a picture of the salvation we experience under the covenant of grace. List what is true of us before salvation, God's work on our behalf, and what is true of us after salvation.

BEFORE SALVATION	GOD'S WORK	AFTER SALVATION

The promises of God are dependent on Him and not on us. What tendencies do you see in your own life to act as if they depend on you? How would resting in that truth change the way you approach your current circumstances?

How can focusing on eternity shift your perspective today?

Christ Fulfills the Covenant of Works

Read Romans 5:12-21

Christ is the fulfillment of every covenant. As the story of Scripture unfolds, God's plan of redemption is progressively revealed through each covenant that God administers, all of them pointing to Jesus, the One who is the yes to every divine promise (2 Corinthians 1:20).

Although those who are in Christ are no longer judged under the covenant of works, but under the covenant of grace. Eternal life still requires perfect obedience to God's holy commands. Life with God still requires unblemished righteousness. It is impossible for sinful man to fulfill the covenant of works, but those who are under the covenant of grace are not judged by their works, but by the works of Christ. He perfectly fulfills the righteous requirements of the covenant of works, and by God's grace through faith, Christ's righteousness is credited to those who believe.

Under the covenant of works, Adam was the covenant head, the representative for all of humanity. Through Adam's one sin, all of humanity became sinful, and that one trespass brought condemnation—the curse of death put forth in the covenant of works—for all people. But the good news is that for those who put their faith in Christ, Adam is no longer our covenant representative. While Adam failed to perfectly follow the covenant of works, Jesus Christ, who is fully God and fully man, perfectly fulfilled its requirements. He lived a life that was completely sinless and fully righteous. Through faith in Him, Christ becomes our new representative. What is true of the covenant head is true of those whom He represents, so just as all were sinful through Adam, we who put our faith in Christ are righteous through Him. Through the first Adam we inherit death, but through Christ we inherit life. Because of Adam's sin, we were separated from God, but because of Christ's obedience, we are reconciled to Him. Christ paid the penalty for our sin in His death and fulfilled the righteous requirement of the covenant of works on our behalf. Our hopeless situation finds hope in Christ.

In order for the covenant of works to be fulfilled, the curse of the covenant had to be satisfied. The holiness of God necessitates just punishment for sin, which means that grace does not come without a cost. Christ not only fulfilled the terms of the covenant, but He also became the curse of the covenant. He absorbed the wrath of God against sin by dying on the cross so that we would be free to receive His righteousness. Grace may be free to us, but it cost Jesus His very life. The cost of our redemption is far more valuable than anything this world can offer and too great a price for us to ever pay. The cost of our salvation was the most precious blood of Christ, the holy and sinless Son of God. In an incredible act of love, God made a way for the covenant of redemption, a covenant

instituted before the foundations of the world, to be fulfilled. God would be faithful to His covenant even when it meant the torturous death of His holy and beloved Son. In fact, in His great love, He set forth Christ's death as the plan from the beginning, knowing full well that the cost of our sin would be the suffering of the Son (Ephesians 1:3-9).

Ever since the first gospel in Genesis 3:15, all of humanity is judged under one of two covenants—the covenant of works or the covenant of grace. By default, all people are represented by the first covenant head, Adam, and thus all are condemned under the covenant curse, but for those who place their faith in Christ, He becomes their new covenant head, and they are now judged on the basis of Christ's righteousness instead of their own. When we place our faith in the perfect righteousness of Jesus Christ, we are justified, legally declared righteous under our perfectly righteous representative. We were all on one path under the covenant of works, barreling toward death after the pattern of our federal head, Adam. But Adam was not the perfect representative we all need, he was only a type of the One to come. Scripture is filled with types—fallible people in Scripture who point to Christ as the One we truly need. They are shadows, imperfect and sinful images of the perfect and sinless Messiah. Adam pointed to the better covenant head, Christ. While Adam's one sin brought death for all people, the death of One—Jesus Christ—brings abundant grace and life for man. For those who put their faith in Him, we are on a different path, a path toward everlasting life. What grace that Jesus would give His life to change the trajectory of ours, and that abundant grace should compel us to share it with others—to invite them to take on a new covenant head—to see the choice set before them and choose life rather than death. How could we not share this incredible news that has been offered to us?

If we are in Christ, the striving ceases. We no longer have to work to gain salvation that we could never earn, because He has earned it for us. As those whom He represents, we become one with Him, and all that is true of Him—His righteousness, His goodness, His holiness—is true of us as well.

What similarities and differences do you see between Adam and Jesus Christ? How does Adam point to Christ as the true and better Adam?

....

....

....

....

....

Read Ephesians 3:1-10. How does God's eternal plan to redeem us through Christ impact your understanding of God's grace and love?

....

....

....

....

....

Are you under the covenant of works or the covenant of grace? If you are in Christ and under the covenant of grace, how do you see tendencies in your own life to live as if you are still under the covenant of works?

....

....

....

....

....

....

God's Covenant with Noah

Read Genesis 6 – 9:17

God will be faithful to His covenant.

As the story of Scripture continues through Genesis, God forms another covenant that is an administration of the overarching covenant of grace. This time the covenant is mediated not by Adam, but by Noah. When Adam and Eve broke the covenant of works, God sent them out of the garden into a world that would bear the effects of the covenant curse. Even so, God had already set in motion His plan to redeem His people and His creation as He covenanted to do in the covenant of redemption. Even though all who live under the covenant of grace are justified in Christ, we still live in bodies and a world marked by the curse, a curse whose power was broken by the cross but whose effects will not be erased until the second coming of Christ.

As soon as Adam broke the covenant, sin and its effects began spreading rapidly throughout the world. The first murder occurs just one generation after Adam and Eve, an incident that would by no means be an isolated one. The depravity of man grows more and more evident as sin spreads like an infectious disease, leaving a trail of death wherever it goes. Genesis 6:5 gives a picture of the pervasiveness of sin after the fall: wickedness so rampant that every single thought and intention of the heart of man is purely evil all the time. God sees the evil that has spread throughout the world—the world He created and called good and the people He made to reflect His own image—and He grieves the outcome of a world that has departed from His created order. He mourns the consequences of the broken covenant, and He resolves to blot out wicked man from the face of the earth. Sin always merits the judgment of God, and the intensity and scope of the judgment of the flood illuminate the pervasiveness and severity of sin. The flood would blot out all of humanity and destroy all life on earth, as every corner of creation is infected by sin. In exercising judgment and wiping out the sin-infected world, God in his grace protects His creation from the destructiveness of sin.

Even in the midst of great sin and great judgment, God does not forget His covenant. God would enact His righteous judgment on a world tainted by sin, but even still, God shows grace. Genesis 6:8 reveals that in the midst of God's pronouncement of judgment, Noah finds favor with God, and the word favor is more often translated as grace. This favor is not based on any goodness that Noah possesses, but purely on God's unmerited grace. In fact, as early as Genesis 9 the Bible shows evidence of Noah's own sinfulness and the effects of his drunkenness, and it is not until after God pronounces His grace upon Noah that Noah is described as righteous, a title bestowed on all who receive the grace of God through faith in the Messiah. In fact, Hebrews 11:7 confirms that Noah's righteousness came not by being sinless, but by faith. The story of Noah presents God's judgment on sin in response to man's breaking of the covenant along with God's grace despite the sinfulness of man as He remains faithful to His covenant, a pattern that will continue throughout the entirety of Scripture. Man's faithlessness does not negate God's faithfulness. God's *hesed*—His covenant faithfulness of love and mercy to His own—will never fail. Through Noah and the covenant God will make with Him, God advances His purposes of grace and redemption.

God sends a flood upon the earth to destroy all life, but He saves Noah and his family, as well as animals to repopulate the earth after the flood. Genesis 8:1 says that God remembered Noah. This terminology does not imply that God forgot about him, but remembered is a term used repeatedly throughout Scripture to describe God's faithfulness to act on behalf of His promises. So God causes the flood to cease and the waters to dry up. When God brings Noah out of the ark, He makes a covenant with Noah. It is clear from this covenant that God intends to fulfill His original purpose for the world since the dawn of creation—a world filled with God's image bearers to reflect His glory in His created order. He promises to never again destroy the earth and cut off all life with the waters of the flood. God does not intend to forfeit His plan for the world because of human sin. This covenant is not just between God and Noah, but includes all of the animals and beasts of the earth, showing God's intention to preserve not just His people, but His creation and created order. He also gives commands to Noah and his family, recommissioning them to do the work that He called Adam and Eve to do in the garden, not as terms for their salvation, but as a means to glorify God. God repeats the familiar command to be fruitful, multiply, and fill the earth. He tells Noah that all the animals will be subject to him, echoing God's command to Adam and Eve to rule and have dominion over the earth.

The Noahic covenant and all future covenants administered by God show the outworking and advancement of the overarching covenant of grace. In God's first administration of the covenant of grace with Adam and Eve, He promised a savior who would come from the seed of the woman, an offspring who would crush the head of the serpent and save God's people from the covenant curse. Now in the Noahic covenant, God promises to preserve humankind, from which will come the promised Messiah, thus protecting the promised seed. Leading up to the fall, the world was in a state of unspeakably wretched sinfulness. But God remains faithful to His covenant. No matter how bad things get, no matter what wickedness abounds in the world, God's plan of redemption will not be thwarted. God will show mercy. God will redeem and restore. God will be faithful to His covenant.

When God makes His covenant with Noah, He offers a sign of the covenant that serves as a reminder of God's faithfulness to keep His promise. The sign is a rainbow that God hangs in the clouds. The word for rainbow is the same word used to describe a weapon of war. In hanging his bow in the sky, God hangs up His weapon and withholds His wrath against the earth so that He can fulfill His covenant of grace. The rainbow serves not only as a reminder of God's promise to sustain the earth until the end, but also of His mercy toward us in withholding the wrath that our sin merits while He patiently waits for repentance. As those who are under God's covenant of grace, we can go forth in the confident hope that God will be merciful and faithful to us despite our sin and the evil around us.

What does the flood reveal about God's character and about human nature?

....

....

....

....

....

....

....

How does God's covenant with Noah advance the purposes of the covenant of grace?

....

....

....

....

....

....

....

....

How does God's preservation of Noah give you hope in the midst of your own failures?

....

....

....

....

....

....

....

— WEEK 2 —

For you are saved by grace through faith, and this is not from yourselves; it is God's gift—not from works, so that no one can boast.

Ephesians 2:8-9

— DAY 6 —

Week Two *Reflection*

Answer the following questions about this week's Scripture passages.

How did the text increase your understanding of covenants?

....
....
....
....
....

What did you observe about God's character?

....
....
....
....
....

What did you learn about the condition of mankind and about yourself?

....
....
....
....
....

How does the text point to the gospel?

....
....
....
....
....
....

How should you respond to this week's text? What is the practical application?

....
....
....
....
....
....

What specific action steps can you take this week to apply the text?

....
....
....
....
....
....

Christ Fulfills the Noahic Covenant

Read Romans 5:1-11, 1 Peter 3:18-22, 2 Peter 3:1-12

Though this world is not as it should be, God's work here is not done.

The flood destroyed all but eight people in God's massive judgment against sin, but the overwhelming waters did not eliminate sin on the earth. Because of God's faithfulness to the covenant of grace, He spared Noah and his family, and because Noah is sinful just like every other human, sin continued to spread. The widespread effects of sin are abundantly clear throughout Scripture and in the world today, and the story leaves no question as to whether or not sin necessitates judgment. In his second letter, Peter warns that the wrath of God revealed in the account of the flood points forward to a second judgment, not by water but by fire, when the sins of men will be punished. This judgment will be ushered in by the second coming of Jesus Christ.

While Christ ushers in God's just judgment against sin, He is also the answer to our sin problem. As sinful humans, we are enemies of God, committing terrible offenses against God and His holiness as we mar His image in ourselves. Because sin must be dealt with and holiness must be restored, we are all rightly subject to the wrath of God. But in Christ, though we were God's enemies, Christ reconciles us to God to make us His children. In Christ's death on the cross, He takes on our sin and receives the judgment due to us. He atones for our sin as our substitute by absorbing the wrath of God, the wrath that was rightly ours, so that we might have His righteousness and so that sin does not go unpunished. The death of Jesus Christ, then, is the means by which God fulfills His covenant promise to preserve and sustain the earth, and specifically, to save His people from His wrath. We can be spared from divine judgment only because Christ takes the judgment for us.

When Noah exited the ark, before God declared His covenant with Noah, Noah set up an altar and made sacrifices to God. He took animals and offered them as burnt offerings to God. Genesis 8 says that the sacrifice was a pleasing aroma to God, and it is in response to the sacrifice that the Lord vowed not to destroy all life again. He did not make the promise that sin had been eliminated from the earth. Rather, God vowed to withhold the fullness of His wrath despite the sinfulness of the human heart. He creates, He sustains, and He saves out of grace. The small sacrifice that Noah made was not enough to atone for His sins, much less the sins of humanity, but it points to the greater sacrifice. Jesus Christ is the once for all sacrifice, the perfect offering that atones for all the sins of God's people, from Adam to us, and beyond. He is the righteous One in 1 Peter 3 who suffers once for the sins of the unrighteous. It is because of this great sacrifice that we are able to experience mercy and grace, without which we would receive the wrath of God. The fullness of that wrath is laid upon Christ, and we, in turn, receive the blessings of the covenant, fulfilled in the righteousness of Christ. Just as Noah and His family were delivered through the floodwaters to safety, we too are delivered through sin and suffering to God.

The covenant God made with Noah was also a covenant with all living things on earth. The scope of this covenant points forward to the scope of what Christ will accomplish on earth. Christ's redemptive work is not limited to sinful humans, but His restoration encompasses all of creation. Christ will return and bring forth judgment, but He will also bring about restoration. The hope of eternity is not just that we will live on this earth forever, but that we will have eternal life in the new heaven and new earth, a renewed and restored home, a home where God dwells with us. We hope not just in God withholding His wrath, but in the restoration of His created order. In the Noahic covenant, God advances His plan to restore what was lost in Eden and renew His creation. In this promise, God's covenant of grace begins to unfold in a way that has not yet been realized fully.

The Noahic covenant is widespread, encompassing all of creation, but it is also particular. God chose Noah, a sinful man out of all the other sinful men on earth, to continue His covenant of grace. God's covenant with Noah also reveals that God works to redeem His people through family. God not only saved Noah, but his family. Because of Christ, we can become part of the family of God, not by mere DNA, which is insufficient to save, but by the blood of Christ that makes us sons of God. Our families in this world are broken and imperfect, but God saves us into a family of sinners turned saints. He redeems a people for Himself, whom He is sanctifying day by day and will ultimately glorify in total sinlessness at Christ's second coming. We look forward to the day when we will be joined together with the entire family of God, made up of people from every tribe, tongue, and nation, worshiping our true Father for all of eternity.

For now, we live in the tension of the already but not yet. We rejoice in the God who gives and sustains life and we exult in the faithfulness of God as the rhythm of seasons carries on and the sun never fails to rise and fall in God's ordained time, but we also mourn as the fruit of the ground and the fruits of our labor become entangled by weeds and sin and thorns. The Noahic covenant reminds us that though this world is not as it should be, God's work here is not done.

How does the flood point forward to Christ's first and second coming?

How does the death of Christ show both the wrath of God and the grace of God?

The Noahic covenant includes not only Noah and his family, but also all of creation. How does this truth give you hope in a broken world?

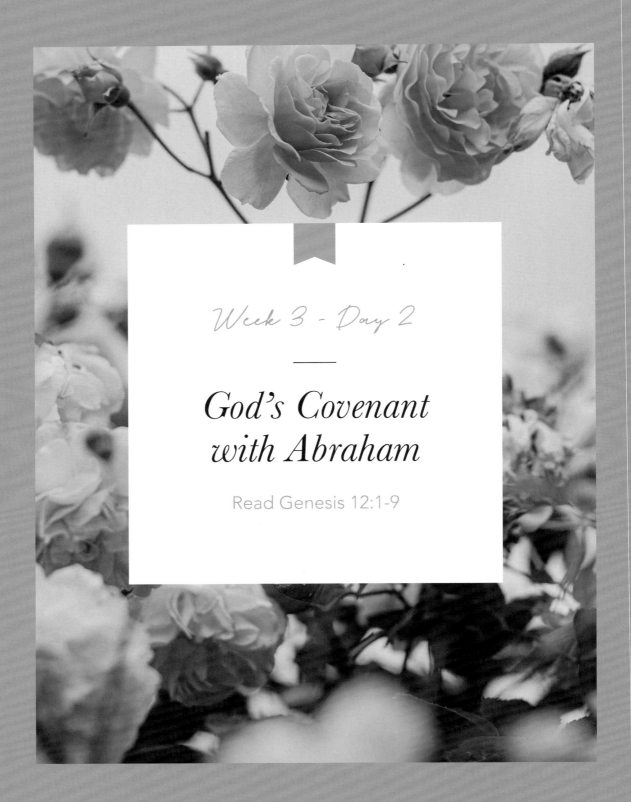

Week 3 - Day 2

—

God's Covenant with Abraham

Read Genesis 12:1-9

> *The entire story of the Bible is the story of God bringing His people to Himself.*

After the flood, the survivors in Noah's family began to multiply until generations and generations of people had been born. It becomes clear very quickly that the flood did not eradicate sin, but that the depravity of man spread from Noah and his family to future generations. Many people were settling in the land of Shinar. They decided to build a tower tall enough to reach the heavens and they set out to make a name for themselves. God gave humankind the purpose of glorifying Him from the beginning, but those who built this great city and tower sought to glorify themselves rather than Him. In order to frustrate their sinful plans and prevent further problems, God changed their language, causing them to scatter in order to live among those with whom they could communicate.

Many generations later, a man named Abram and his family enter the story in Genesis 11. They are from Ur of the Chaldeans, a pagan nation, and they worship false gods (Joshua 24:2-3). Abram has a wife named Sarai who is barren, childless, and without hope of off-spring. As unlikely a candidate as Abram may be, God will use him to advance His plan of redemption and His covenant of grace to His people. That is the way God works. He calls out sinners to make them saints, He uses the weak to shame the strong, and He lifts up the lowly to exalt them. Abram is no exception. And so God calls Abram to leave Ur and to journey to Canaan. Under the leadership of Terah, his pagan father, they only make it to Haran and settle there instead. Terah dies in Haran, but God has not forgotten Abram.

In Genesis 12, God appears to Abram after the death of his father and calls him to go once again to the land that He would show him. God enters into a covenant with Abram, not only to bring Abram near, but an entire people who are far from God. This covenant is another administration of God's overarching covenant of grace, and it is a crucial point in redemptive history as God reveals with new clarity His plan to redeem His people. In the Abrahamic covenant, God makes several promises to Abram that can be categorized into three larger promises.

First, God promises Abram a people. God says that He will give Abram a great name and make him a great nation. This promise would be a remarkable promise to anyone, but the circumstances of Abram's life make it all the more incredible. He has no children, and his wife is barren. From this couple would come countless offspring. God tells Abram in Genesis 13 that he will have so many descendants that they will be like the dust of the earth—innumerable. The covenant curse of sin brought death and pain, and Abram and Sarai experience the effects of that curse firsthand. Apart from God's promises, their family, their inheritance, their name—all of it would die with them. But God promises to bring life where there is none, to bring redemption and restoration from fallen creation, and He promises to do it through Abram.

God also promises Abram a land. God calls him once again to go to the land that He will show him and He promises to give it to Abram and his offspring. This land will be a home for Abram's family, for the great nation that he would become, but more than that, it will be a place where God's people will dwell in His presence. When God pronounced the curse of the covenant of works on Adam and Eve, He sent them out of the garden and away from the presence of God. Sin results in separation from God. But now God comes to Abram and commands him to go, not away from God's presence, but into God's presence. In God's loving kindness under the covenant of grace, He is working to bring His own home. The entire story of the Bible is the story of God bringing His people to Himself, a story of God redeeming sinners to be His children and restoring His presence to His people. The Bible is the story of God bringing His people home to dwell with Him as their God.

God also promises Abram abundant blessing that will not only be for himself, but for all the nations of the world. Where we earned curses by our sin, God promises covenant blessings. God promises His grace, His unmerited favor, to those who merited only death. Abram is no exception. He is a man who worshiped pagan idols, and even after God makes His covenant with Abram, it is clear that he still battles sin and doubt in his own life, but He who promises is faithful. God will bless Abram, but God's plans for blessing in His covenant of grace extend far beyond this man. Through Abram, we are blessed, and God's plan for Abram's offspring continues to unfold in the pages of His Word.

He calls out sinners to make them saints, He uses the weak to shame the strong, and He lifts up the lowly and exalts them.

*How do God's promises to Abram advance the promise He made
to Adam and Eve in Genesis 3?*

....

....

....

....

....

....

*God called Abram out of a life of worshiping other gods to follow Him. How are
you like Abram in worshiping idols of power, pride, people, or pleasure?*

....

....

....

....

....

....

....

*Between Abram's pagan family and barren wife, he seemed like an unlikely candidate
to receive the promises of God. How were you an unlikely candidate to receive
God's grace? What does God's choice to save Abram and you reveal about
God's character and the way that He works?*

....

....

....

....

....

....

Waiting on the Promise

Read Genesis 1–5

God's ability to fulfill His promises is not dependent on circumstances.

God made big promises to Abram, but they did not come true overnight. God would be faithful and He would fulfill those promises in His perfect timing.

In Genesis 15, God comes to Abram once again and assures him that He would indeed bless Abram greatly just as He promised. As God repeats His promises to Abram, he cries out to the Lord in his waiting asking, "What can you give me?" God promised Abraham descendants too numerous to count, but Abram does not even have one child. How can God give him what He promised when his circumstances are all wrong? The heir of all of his wealth is not even from his own family, but is a servant in his household. There does not seem to be a solution to this obstacle.

God does not leave Abram alone in his waiting. God comes to Abram and reminds him of His covenant. God confirms to Abram that his heir would be his own son—his own flesh and blood. God's ability to fulfill His promises is not dependent on circumstances. Nothing is too hard for the Lord. As God leads Abram out under the sky He tells him to look up and count the stars. The night sky that Abram sees is not like the night sky we might see now, but it is a sky free of light pollution, filled with so many stars that it would be impossible to keep track of them all. Even with today's incredibly advanced technology, scientists have not been able to number the stars in the heavens. Even so, God does not alter His promise based on Abram's circumstance, He confirms it. God is able, no matter how big the promise.

God not only reminds Abram of the promises of blessing and offspring, but also of the promise of land. When Abram asks how he will know that God will give him the land He promised, God tells Abram to do something that may seem strange. He tells him to bring animals and cut them in half. Although this concept may seem foreign and bizarre to the contemporary reader, it would have been very familiar to the original audience. What God asks Abram to do is typical of ancient near-eastern covenant ceremonies. In these ceremonies, animals would be cut in half and the parties entering into the covenant would walk between the pieces. This ceremony represents a self-maledictory oath, which is an oath that someone takes against themselves, declaring that if it is broken, they will take on the negative consequences themselves. In this ceremony, the less powerful party, known as a vassal, vows to receive a curse if he does not uphold the terms of the covenant. As he walks through the divided animals, the lesser party symbolically states, "so may God do to me and more also if I fail to keep the terms of this covenant." A covenant is not a simple promise, but a bond in blood, an oath made with life or death implications.

When Genesis 15:19 says that God "made a covenant," the Hebrew is *karath berit*, which literally means to cut a covenant, a phrase commonly used throughout Scripture to indicate the beginning of a covenant, language that recalls this gruesome ceremony.

Abram cuts the animals in half as God commands and then he waits. Rather than telling Abram to walk through the divided pieces as would have been customary, God puts Abram into a deep sleep when the sun sets. The Lord tells Abram that he will indeed have offspring and a land, but that the journey to the promise will not be easy. They will live in slavery in a foreign nation, but God will deliver them and give them great possessions. The road to promise may be marked with suffering, but the blessings on the other side will be far greater than any pain along the way.

While the initial elements of a covenant ceremony would have been familiar to early readers, what happens next is shocking. A smoking oven and a flaming torch pass between the pieces, representing God Himself completing the covenant ceremony. This scene is remarkable because in a covenant it is always the lesser party, the servant of the greater lord, who takes on the covenant curse if he should disobey. Incredibly, it is not Abram who bears the responsibility of the covenant curse, but God who takes the self-maledictory oath. God walks through the divided animals alone, bearing the full weight of the curse. This covenant ceremony is a picture of the God who takes on the role of the servant for those who should rightly serve Him. It points to the Messiah who becomes a curse for His people, bearing the weight of their sin, and dying in their place. Abram, like all people, is unable to walk in perfect faithfulness and obedience, but the promises of God are not dependent on sinful humans, but on Him. The covenant of grace is secured because it is God who cuts the covenant, it is God who carries it out, and it is God who pays the penalty of the curse. When God enters into covenant with His people, He enters into a binding, unbreakable oath, and He can be trusted to fulfill every single one.

Abram waited on the promise, and the waiting was not easy. He became frustrated and weary, wondering how God could ever be faithful to such an impossible promise. But Abram believed God. Even when it was difficult, Abram had faith that God would fulfill His promises. His faith wavered and he would doubt once again, but God was faithful to work faith in him, and He is faithful to work faith in us. Cling to His promises. Cling to His character. Even in the waiting, He is faithful.

God would be faithful and He would fulfill those
promises in His perfect timing.

Read Galatians 3:13. How does the covenant ceremony in Genesis 15 point to what Paul says about Christ in this verse?

....
....
....
....
....
....

Have you ever had to trust God in a season of waiting?
How can Abram's story bring encouragement and hope in your waiting?

....
....
....
....
....
....

God does not leave us alone in our waiting, but gives us Himself, His Word, and His people to remind us of who He is and what He has done. What are some practical ways you can remind yourself of God's faithfulness in your season of waiting?

....
....
....
....
....
....

Week 3 - Day 4

—

He is
Faithful Still

Read Genesis 17

Even in our waiting, let us look to the God who is able.

It does not take long after God confirms His covenant with Abram in Genesis 15 for Abram to take matters into his own hands. In Genesis 16, Abram and Sarai are still childless, and Sarai proposes a plan. Abram would sleep with an Egyptian servant in their household named Hagar so that she would have a son for Abram. Abram and Sarai desire the promises of God, but they have a difficult time trusting in God's way and time. Abram sleeps with Hagar and she becomes pregnant and gives birth to a baby boy named Ishmael when Abram is 86 years old, sixteen years after God called him in Genesis 12. Perhaps Abram and Sarai think that the years of waiting are finally over, even if things didn't turn out quite like they hoped, but God still has better plans for them.

There is a thirteen year gap between the birth of Ishmael and the beginning of Genesis 17. God appears to Abram once again at the age of 99 and confirms the covenant He originally made with him. When God appears to Abram, the first thing He says is "I Am God Almighty." Abram may have given up on having a son with Sarai, but God reminds Abram who He is. He is the all powerful, almighty, sovereign God. Nothing is impossible for Him. He is the God who promised and is willing and able to fulfill that promise completely. God reminds Abram that he can trust in God's promises because he knows His character.

God does not diminish His promise to Abram in light of his circumstances, but expands it. In the past God had promised to make Abram a great nation, and now He promises to make him the father of a multitude of nations. God changes his name from Abram, which means exalted father, to Abraham, which means father of a multitude of nations. In God's great plan, the one who was childless would be called the father of many. After years of fruitlessness, God would make Abraham exceedingly fruitful. The covenant that God made with Abraham is everlasting and extends to Abraham and his offspring, offspring that at this time did not yet exist, offspring that Abraham dared not dream of before God promised them to him. His offspring would have the land of Canaan, the promised land, and God would dwell there with them as their God. In God's upside-down kingdom, the lowly are exalted, the weak are crowned with strength, and all that is lost is restored.

God then gives Abraham a sign of the covenant. Abraham, his male offspring, and all the males in his household are to be circumcised. This sign is not a saving act, but a reminder of God's promises to Abraham. It is not a condition of the covenant, but a sign of being part of the covenant community. Like the rainbow in the sky that reminds God's people of His promise not to destroy the earth again with water after the flood, God gives Abraham a sign that He will be faithful to fulfill His promises of countless offspring who

will dwell with God, carved into the very organ that brings forth those offspring. It is an ever-present reminder that God will be faithful, even when the fulfillment of His promises remains unseen.

God has not forgotten His covenant, and He has not forgotten Sarai. Just as Abraham received a new name, God gives Sarai a new name too. Sarai is now Sarah, and God gives her the same promises that He gave Abraham. Nations will come from her, just as they will from Abraham. God promises to bless her just as He promised to bless Abraham. God once again promises Abraham a son, not from Hagar, but from Sarah. Abraham's reaction is to be expected for someone receiving the news that his 90 year old barren wife would have a child. He laughs at the prospect of a woman who not only suffered from infertility, but is now well beyond child-bearing years, becoming pregnant and having a child. Abraham proposes a different plan, that Ishmael, the son he fathered through Hagar, would be the recipient of the covenant, but God responds by saying that Abraham's own son through Sarah would be his heir, and that the covenant that God made with Abraham would be established through that son. This son would be born one year later and his name would be Isaac. God would make a way for His promises to be fulfilled to His people.

Abraham has not yet seen the promise of the covenant fulfilled, but he still steps out in obedience because he believes the promises of God. He and his household are circumcised that very day, a sign of God's faithfulness to fulfill every promise, even the ones that seem impossible. We may find ourselves waiting on the promises of God, wondering how He could ever show up. Even in our waiting, let us look to the God who is able, the Almighty God who keeps covenant and steadfast love with His people, and let us step out in obedience and faithfulness to Him as we wait.

When God appears to Abram in Genesis 17, He begins by reminding Abram who He is before reminding him of His promises. How can God's character give you confidence in His promises?

....

....

....

....

....

....

What promises of God do you struggle to believe? How does God's faithfulness to Abram and Sarai encourage your faith?

....

....

....

....

....

....

What would it look like for you to walk in obedience while you wait on the Lord right now?

....

....

....

....

....

....

Christ Fulfills the Abrahamic Covenant

Read Romans 4, Galatians 3:7-14, Hebrews 11:8-16

We have faith in the unseen because we have faith in the God who promises.

God made grand and glorious promises to Abraham in the Abrahamic covenant, and though they would be fulfilled in part during his lifetime and his children's lifetime, they will ultimately be fulfilled in Jesus Christ.

One of the promises God made to Abraham in His covenant was the promise that through Abraham, all the nations of the world would be blessed. God promised Abraham a seed—an offspring—and it is because of that seed that the world would find blessing through Abraham. Tracing through the line of Abraham's descendants reveals that Jesus Christ is born from Abraham's lineage. Paul argues in Romans 4 and Galatians 3 that all those who have faith in the Messiah, Jesus Christ, receive the blessing promised to Abraham in the covenant instead of the curse of the covenant of works. Redemption from the covenant curse is only possible because Christ became a curse for us by dying on the cross. When God passed between the divided animals in Genesis 15 assuring Abraham that He would fulfill the promises of the covenant He made with him, God swore an oath to take the covenant curse upon Himself rather than place it on His servants. Jesus Christ—the second person of the trinity, the Son of God, God incarnate—fulfills that promise by humbling Himself to the position of a servant and dying in our place. The curse of the covenant is broken because Christ bore it, and the blessing of the covenant is secured because Christ earned it. This blessing we receive by faith.

Among the blessings given to Abraham is the promise that God would make him a great nation. While Abraham saw the beginnings of this promise fulfilled, it is in Christ that Abraham's descendants are multiplied beyond his bloodline. In Romans 4, Paul makes the argument that Abraham's true offspring, the ones who would inherit the promises of God's covenant with Abraham, are not those who share his DNA, but those who share his faith. To be a child of Abraham means to receive the blessing of the covenant the same way Abraham did—by faith in the promised Messiah. When God restated the promises of the covenant in Genesis 15, Scripture says that Abraham believed the promises of God and his faith was counted to him as righteousness. He was credited with a righteousness that he did not earn.

The same is true of those who are in Christ. When sinners believe the promise of God to save, to redeem them from the covenant curse, and bring them under the covenant of grace, He takes on their sin, paying its penalty on the cross, and gives them His righteousness, the righteousness required to receive the blessing of the covenant. In Christ, countless people from every tribe, tongue, and nation enter into new life under the covenant of grace and receive the promises given to Abraham and his offspring. In Christ, Abraham becomes the father not just of Jews, but of Gentiles. In Christ, those who were far off can be included in God's people. In Christ, Abram becomes Abraham — the father of a multitude of nations.

Jesus not only brings about the promises of countless offspring and blessing for the nations, but also the promise of a land for the people to dwell with God in perfect peace. God eventually delivered Abraham's offspring into the promised land of Canaan, but their stay there was cut short by exile and destruction. God's promise that His people would live in the land eternally is not lost. Instead, all God's redeemed, like Abraham, look forward to the new and true promised land, the future homeland, a city that God has prepared for His people. We long not for a place we can see now, but a better, heavenly country. We have not yet seen it, but we have faith in the unseen because we have faith in the God who promises. We long for the day when Jesus Christ returns and ushers in the new creation, the glorious and everlasting promised land where God Himself will dwell with us as our God, and we will dwell with Him as His people. Christ has made a way for us to return to His presence, to dwell with our holy God whom we call Father because of the blood of Christ.

Jesus Christ is the blessed seed of Abraham who brings many sons into the blessing of the covenant of grace. Jesus Christ multiplies Abraham's offspring by faith in His work to fulfill the covenant. Jesus Christ declares us fit to be in God's presence and will bring the promised land down from heaven to us. When Abraham hoped in the promise of the covenant, Abraham hoped in Jesus Christ, and we share that same hope.

*How does Jesus Christ fulfill the promises of blessing for the nations,
a people, and a land?*

BLESSING	PEOPLE	LAND

*By what means did Abraham receive the blessings of the covenant?
Does it differ from how we receive the blessings of the covenant today?*

....
....
....
....
....
....

*Read Revelation 21:1-4. How is the New Jerusalem—the true promised land—the
better fulfillment of God's promise to give Abraham a homeland?*

....
....
....
....
....
....
....

— WEEK 3 —

Abram believed the Lord, and he credited it to him as righteousness.

Genesis 15:6

— DAY 6 —

Week Three *Reflection*

Answer the following questions about this week's Scripture passages.

How did the text increase your understanding of covenants?

....
....
....
....
....

What did you observe about God's character?

....
....
....
....
....

What did you learn about the condition of mankind and about yourself?

....
....
....
....
....

How does the text point to the gospel?

....

....

....

....

....

....

How should you respond to this week's text? What is the practical application?

....

....

....

....

....

....

What specific action steps can you take this week to apply the text?

....

....

....

....

....

....

The Promise Passed Down

Read Genesis 21:1-7, Genesis 22, Genesis 26:1-5,
Genesis 28:10-16, Genesis 35:9-15

When God makes a promise,
He always follows through.

After decades of waiting, God gave Abraham and Sarah the son He promised them. This son was named Isaac, and he would be the child of the covenant as God promised. God did just as He said He would do exactly when He said He would do it, and even though Abraham and Sarah waited years to see the answer to the promise of a son, God's answer was right on time. God is never late. He is not slow to fulfill His promises (2 Peter 3:9), but even in the waiting, God is working.

The promise of the covenant was to continue through Isaac's line, but even after Isaac's birth, Abraham's need for faith does not diminish. God tests Abraham's faith when He asks him to sacrifice his only son Isaac, the child of promise. This is the one through whom Abraham's offspring would be named, the hope of blessing for all the nations of the world, and now God asks Abraham to sacrifice him before Isaac ever gives Abraham his first grandson. If Abraham were to obey God, wouldn't the promise God made to him be obsolete? Wouldn't it be impossible for God to fulfill His promise to carry the covenant through Isaac if Isaac were dead? But Abraham knows that nothing is too hard for the Lord (Genesis 18:14). Hebrews 11 says that Abraham had such faith in God's promise to make Abraham a great nation through Isaac that he was willing to obey God, believing that God could raise Isaac from the dead to keep His covenant. Instead of requiring Abraham to offer up his only son to death, God provides a way for Isaac to escape death. God provides another sacrifice to take Isaac's place and die in his stead. God does the same for us. The Father sends His only Son to die in our place so that we might receive the blessing of the covenant with Abraham. God would offer His only Son as the perfect sacrifice, and would raise His only Son from the dead, securing the blessings of the promise through the promised seed.

God restates His covenant with Abraham once again, declaring that He will fulfill the promises He made to Abraham because of His obedience. If God's covenant requires obedience, how then is it a covenant of grace? How is it not a covenant of works? The covenant of grace does still require perfect obedience—righteousness before God—but the grace of God is that He is the One who fulfills the righteous requirement and produces that righteousness in His redeemed. Abraham was not righteous because of his own perfect obedience or holiness. In fact, evidence of Abraham's sin is woven all throughout the account of his life in the book of Genesis. Abraham had no righteousness of his own, but because he believed that God would fulfill the promises He made, God counted his faith as righteousness. Abraham was justified by faith, and to be justified means to be declared to be righteous, to have a positional holiness, a legal right standing before God.

All believers are declared righteous in the same way, by faith in Jesus Christ so that His righteousness is credited to us. Justification always leads to sanctification, the process by which God makes us righteous, working in us the obedience of righteousness that has already been declared to be true of us in Christ. Faith results in good works, and those good works—our obedience to God—are evidence of that saving faith. Abraham was not righteous because he obeyed. Abraham obeyed because of the righteousness that God worked in him. The promises of the covenant of grace are given to those who are righteous by faith, and the promises of the covenant of grace are guaranteed and totally secure because it is God who produces faith and righteousness in us.

Soon after Sarah dies, Isaac marries a woman named Rebekah. Genesis 25 reveals that Rebekah, like Sarah, is barren, but God has already proven that His promises cannot be thwarted. Isaac prays for Rebekah and she conceives twins, Jacob and Esau. In Genesis 26, God appears to Isaac and restates the promises He made to Abraham of offspring more numerous than the stars, blessing for the nations, and a land to dwell in. God continues His covenant through Isaac, just as He promised He would do.

While Rebekah is pregnant, God tells her that her older son, Esau, will serve the younger son, Jacob. It was customary for the oldest son to receive the inheritance of his father, but God had other plans. God intends to make Jacob the heir of the covenant and carry on His promises through Jacob. God makes a habit of using unlikely candidates to advance His kingdom—the weak, the lowly, the barren—so that His power will be made perfect in weakness and His glory will be displayed (2 Corinthians 12:9). Esau, the firstborn, ends up selling his birthright, which is his right to the inheritance, to Jacob for a bowl of stew. Jacob later steals Esau's blessing from Isaac. Jacob's actions are deceitful, but God is not limited by sin. God uses a broken situation to advance His kingdom and carry on His covenant.

In Genesis 28, God appears to Jacob in a dream and gives to him the promises that He gave to Abraham and Isaac. The language of the promises God gives to Abraham, Isaac, and Jacob are consistent, and their continuity reveals that God's covenants are the backbone of His plan of redemption. Through more barrenness and strife, God gives Jacob twelve sons and a new name, Israel. He gives him the same call He gave to Adam and Eve and to Noah, to be fruitful and multiply. He promises once again that nations will come from him, and that the land promised to Abraham and Isaac will be given to him. Jacob's twelve sons become the twelve tribes of Israel.

God's covenant plans cannot be stopped, and His covenant faithfulness will never be undone. Even through generations of bareness and countless acts of sin, God is still faithful. His plans cannot be thwarted. God has always been faithful to fulfill His covenant of redemption and He will be faithful to the end.

How does the sacrifice of Isaac point forward to Jesus Christ?

....

....

....

....

....

....

What does the fact that God continues His covenant through Abraham's offspring reveal about God's character and plan?

....

....

....

....

....

....

What circumstances in your life seem insurmountable? How does God's faithfulness to carry on His promises through brokenness give you hope in your own circumstances?

....

....

....

....

....

....

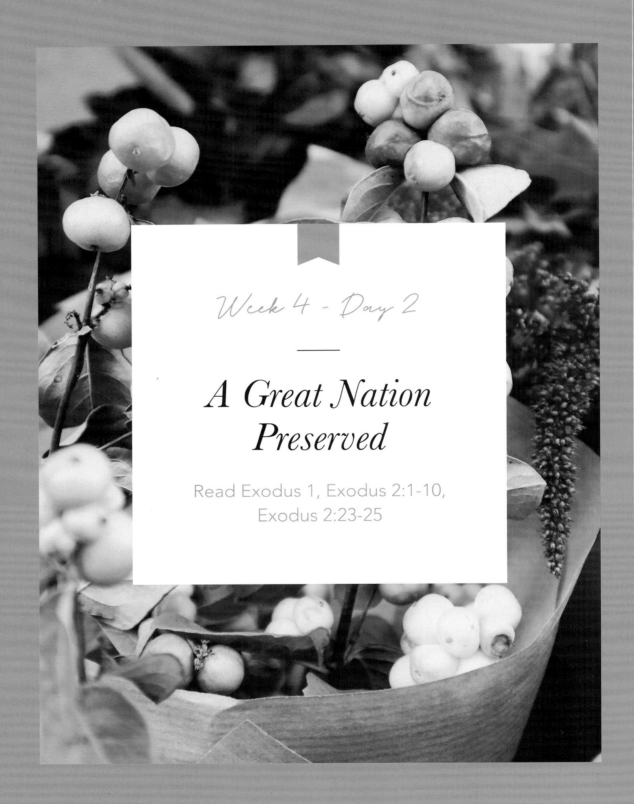

Week 4 - Day 2

—

A Great Nation Preserved

Read Exodus 1, Exodus 2:1-10,
Exodus 2:23-25

But what they meant for evil,
God intended for good.

God's covenant faithfulness to Abraham, Isaac, and Jacob would not stop with them, but would continue on to future generations. Jacob, who was renamed Israel, had twelve sons. Joseph, his first son from Rachel, who had previously been barren, was Jacob's most beloved son, and his brothers resented him for their father's favoritism, even more so when Joseph shared his dreams indicating that he would rule over all his brothers. They wanted him gone, so they faked his death to Israel and sold Joseph into slavery in Egypt. Through a series of incredible, God-ordained events, Joseph rose to power in Pharaoh's household and was placed over all Pharaoh had as his second in command. Joseph went from slavery to a position of near royalty. Leading up to Joseph's rise to power, God had given Pharaoh dreams that were brought before Joseph to interpret. Joseph told him that God was going to send seven years of abundance throughout all of the land of Egypt, followed by seven years of extreme famine, and proposed that Pharaoh store up their crops during the seven years of plenty to prepare for the seven years of famine. When the years of famine arrived, the famine was very severe, not only in Egypt, but throughout the world, and people from all over came to buy grain from Egypt's stores. Israel sent his sons — Joseph's very own brothers — to Egypt to buy food. Joseph recognized his brothers, and instead of taking revenge on them for the evil they had done to him, he welcomed them and showed them mercy, bringing his father and brothers into Egypt and providing for them.

All this time, God never stopped working to fulfill His covenant to Abraham, Isaac, and Jacob. Joseph's brothers intended evil against him, but what they meant for evil, God intended for good (Genesis 50:20). God was working in the midst of Joseph's suffering to preserve the people God promised to Abraham. God sent Joseph ahead of his brothers to Egypt so that through him, God would preserve a remnant for Himself rather than lose them to the famine.

Now the story picks up in the book of Exodus. Chapter 1 opens with clear evidence that God is faithfully working to fulfill His covenant to Abraham, and ultimately, His covenant of grace for all His people. The members of Israel's family who came to Egypt were 70, but this small number was very fruitful and multiplied greatly so that Egypt was filled with Israelites. God's promise to make Abraham's offspring more numerous than the stars is coming true despite barrenness and opposition and famine, and God's original design in Eden to fill the world with His image bearers has not been lost. The Israelites grow so great in number that when a new king rises to power in Egypt, a king who does not know Joseph, he fears the strength of the Israelites and forces them to become slaves. It might seem as if God's covenant to bless His people is falling apart, but God's plans cannot be opposed. In fact, all of this is part of God's plan to fulfill His covenant, and He even told Abraham in Genesis 15 when He performed the covenant ceremony that Abraham's offspring would be slaves in a foreign land for 400 years. This news should come as no surprise, and neither should the result, which God also promised—the people would be delivered and the nation that enslaved them would be judged. God is not surprised by the sorrows of the Israelites and He does not grow anxious as the king's evil plan unfolds, but God is working in every moment to bring about his promises.

In an attempt to weaken the Israelites, the Pharaoh, who is the king of Egypt, orders every Hebrew baby boy to be killed, but no power can come against the power of the Almighty God. The Hebrew midwives who deliver the babies choose to obey the one true God rather than the god of Egypt, and they spare the baby boys who are born to the Israelite women. The narrative introduces a Hebrew woman, a Levite, who gives birth to a baby boy named Moses. She hides him from the Egyptians for three months, all the while fearing that he will be discovered and killed, but she cannot not hide him forever, so she puts him in a basket and hides him among the reeds in the river. The Hebrew word for basket is the same word that is translated ark. God has plans for little Moses—plans to deliver His people through him. God is faithful to preserve His people. Just as God preserved Noah and his family through the waters of destruction in the ark, He will preserve and deliver His people through Moses, the helpless Hebrew baby boy floating in the little ark. Moses is found by none other than Pharaoh's own daughter who adopts him as her own. Moses had a death sentence from birth, but God intended to use him to advance His covenant. Through Moses, God is working to keep His covenant with Abraham, to multiply him and make him a great nation

Years later, Pharaoh dies, and the people cry out to God in the affliction of their slavery seeking deliverance. God hears their groaning, and He remembers His covenant with Abraham, Isaac, and Jacob. God had said that Abraham's offspring would be enslaved for 400 years and then delivered to the promised land, and God will follow through on that promise. All that God would do in the book of Exodus He would do on the precedence of the covenant He made with Abraham.

When we are experiencing suffering, it can feel as if God has turned His back on us, forgotten us, and is blind to our pain, but in the book of Exodus we see a compassionate God who is with us in it all. When the painful groanings of the Israelites rise up to God, He hears them in their distress. When they are victims of injustice, God sees them. When the people of God experience suffering too great to bear, God knows. Through it all, God remembers. He remembers His people. He remembers His promises. He remembers His covenant. The same is true for us today. We worship a God who not only sees and hears our pain but sympathizes with it. Christ bore the full suffering of sin on the cross in our place, and He truly knows the pain we endure. We serve a God who not only is aware of our suffering but is sovereign over it and working in it to bring about our deliverance.

God is on our side, and God is working in every detail, even the difficult ones, to fulfill His glorious promises to us. God is sovereign over our circumstances to bring about the blessings of the covenant of grace for us as His people just as He did for the Israelites. Our God will remember His covenant.

How many times are Abraham, Isaac, and Jacob mentioned in the passages you read? How is God's covenant with Abraham, Isaac, and Jacob connected with the work He will do in Exodus?

....

....

....

....

How do you see God's sovereignty to fulfill His promises in today's reading?

....

....

....

....

How does the knowledge that God hears, sees, knows, and remembers us in our suffering give you encouragement?

....

....

....

....

God's People Delivered

Read Exodus 3, Exodus 6:2-9, Exodus 11,
Exodus 12:1-14, Exodus 14

What is impossible for man is possible with God.

God chose Moses and saved him from death as an infant, but it is not until many years later that God reveals His plan for Moses. In Exodus 3, God calls to Moses from a burning bush. God announces Himself as the God of Abraham, Isaac, and Jacob, making it known that He is the covenant-keeping God who intends to carry out His covenant faithfulness to Abraham. Moses will be an integral part of God's covenant story as God's instrument to bring about His promises. God reveals elements of His character to Moses at the end of chapter 2—God hears, God sees, God knows, and God will deliver. God assures Moses that He intends to deliver the Israelites out of slavery in Egypt and into the promised land, just as He promised Abraham He would do.

God calls Moses to a task that seems far too difficult: to appear before Pharaoh and deliver the Israelites from their slavery in Egypt. Moses' response to God is to be expected. Moses says, "Who am I that I should bring them out?" Moses knows that he does not have the power to complete the task set before him. He has no sway over the hearts of kings. He does not have sufficient wisdom to convince Pharaoh. He has no strength to force his hand. Moses cannot deliver the Israelites, but God can. God's response to Moses is not that Moses is capable or that he is good enough to do it, but instead God assures Moses that He will be with him. Moses may be God's instrument, but God is the One who will do the work. What is impossible for man is possible with God (Luke 18:27).

It is at this point that God does something remarkable—He reveals His name, and in doing so, He reveals His character. God identifies Himself by saying, "I AM WHO I AM." God's name is Yahweh, meaning "I AM." He is the self-existent, self-sufficient, unchanging, eternal God who was and is and is to come. He is the God who keeps covenant with His people. This is the God who sees our affliction, who hears our cries, and who knows our pain, and this is the God who comes down to save. Moses may have felt inadequate to do what God called him to do, but God calls Moses to take his eyes off his own shortcomings and lift His gaze to God. God's answer to Moses' cry of, "Who am I?" is a resounding "I AM." He is the One who is able, and He is the One who does the work. God calls Moses to step out in obedience so that His covenant purposes might be advanced, but God is the One who guarantees that the covenant would be fulfilled.

God tells Moses that Pharaoh will initially refuse Moses' request, but God will send plagues of judgment upon Egypt. God's people often face opposition and rejection in the work that God calls them to do, but God is faithful to make it happen in His time. Just as God said, Pharaoh refuses to let the Israelites go, and moreover, he makes their work as slaves exponentially more difficult. As the people's suffering increases, Moses questions why God would bring evil upon His people when He had promised blessing. Rather than give Moses an explanation, God tells Moses who He is. Over and over again, He states his name, Yahweh, which is written LORD in most English translations. He refers back to His covenant and promises to fulfill it. He will bring them into the land He promised, and He will make them His people and He will be their God.

When Pharaoh refuses to listen to the message that God gave him through Moses, God brings plagues upon Egypt. As Pharaoh's hardness of heart continues, God sends the final plague—the death of the firstborn. God warns that if Pharaoh does not turn and release the Israelites, He will put to death every firstborn in Egypt, whether man or animal. Death is the just judgment that sin deserves, and every unrepentant heart that will not turn to the Lord in faith will receive His wrath. Even in the face of death, God offers His people salvation. God instructs the Israelites to take and kill a lamb without any blemish or imperfection and paint the blood of the lamb around the door frame of their houses, and God would pass over those houses instead of bringing the judgment of death. The Passover is an incredible picture of the pure and spotless Messiah who was to come, whose blood would cover our own sins so that God's judgment might fall on Jesus Christ and pass over us. In the first Passover, God keeps his promise to Abraham by preserving His offspring, and through Jesus, the true Passover lamb, God is preserving those who are Abraham's offspring by faith in Christ.

When the tenth plague strikes, Pharaoh quickly sends the Israelites out of Egypt into the wilderness. The presence of God leads them through the wilderness by a pillar of cloud by day and a pillar of fire by night until they reach the Red Sea. Even after Pharaoh sends them away, God hardens Pharaoh's heart so that he pursues the Israelites with the full strength of his army. The Israelites look up and see a terrifying sight that seems like imminent death marching toward them. With their heels backed up against the Red Sea and more than 600 chariots ready to attack, they cry out in hopeless desperation in anticipation of the tragedy that is to come upon them. But Moses knows who God is, because God has revealed Himself to Moses. Moses knows that He is the great I AM who is stronger than a million armies, who is sovereign over every moment, and who always keeps His covenants. Moses experienced the God of creation, and Moses believes that He will deliver them.

In this life or death moment, God remains true to His character. He sends a wind to part the Red Sea so that the Israelites can walk on dry land, but when the Egyptians pursue them, God sends the waters crashing down on the Egyptians. Just as with Noah, God preserves His people by delivering them through the waters of judgment that come down upon those who are unrepentant. Throughout the Old Testament, God frequently refers to Himself as the God who delivered His people out of slavery. God is a God who delivers His people and brings them to Himself. The exodus points to the greater deliverance found in Christ—the deliverance from slavery to sin — the deliverance from death to life. God's covenants will not fail. He is the God who delivered His people, and He will deliver again.

When we look at the things God has called us to do and feel overwhelmed, saying things like "Who am I to raise these children, to teach these women, to care for my hurting neighbors, to endure this trial?" we are asking the wrong question. We should not be asking, "Who am I?" but "Who is God?" We may not always find the why we are looking for, but the Who is enough. We must remind ourselves of who God is. He is the great I AM. He is able. He is faithful. God is doing a good thing in ways we cannot see. Even in our suffering, we can trust Him to fulfill His promises because of who He is.

Moses knows that he is inadequate to do the work God is calling him to, but God reminds him that He is the One who will do the work. In what areas of your life are you inadequate to do what God has called you to do, and how does the knowledge that God is the One who does the work encourage you?

....

....

....

....

....

....

....

....

....

....

....

....

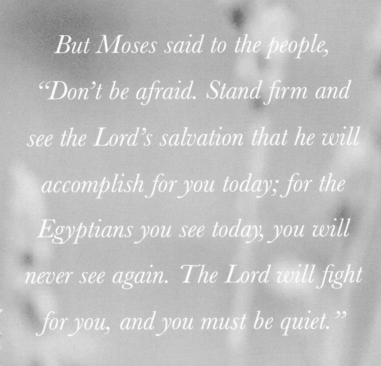

But Moses said to the people,
"Don't be afraid. Stand firm and
see the Lord's salvation that he will
accomplish for you today; for the
Egyptians you see today, you will
never see again. The Lord will fight
for you, and you must be quiet."

———

EXODUS 14:13-14

How does the Passover point forward to God's redemption in Christ?

....
....
....
....
....
....
....

When God appears to Moses in the burning bush, He reveals to Moses who He is and what He promises to do, and Moses is able to encourage the Israelites in the face of great fear (Exodus 14:13-14). God has revealed His character and His promises to us in His Word. How should your knowledge of God and His promises impact the way you face trials in your own life?

....
....
....
....
....
....
....
....
....
....
....
....
....

Week 4 - Day 4

—

God's Covenant with Moses

Exodus 19, Exodus 20:1-21,
Exodus 24:1-8, Deuteronomy 7:6-8

We do not obey in order to earn salvation; we obey because we have been saved.

God delivered the Israelites out of slavery in Egypt, just as He promised. Deuteronomy 7:6-8 reveals that God did not choose the Israelites because they were impressive in any way, but God's choice to redeem them, deliver them from slavery in Egypt, and make them His own people was based purely on His own love and grace and faithfulness to His covenant with Abraham. Now the Israelites find themselves in the wilderness until they come to Mount Sinai. It is there that God will establish His covenant with Israel through Moses as the mediator, a covenant that will expand on the Abrahamic covenant as another administration of the overarching covenant of grace.

A distinguishing element of this covenant that God establishes through Moses is the giving of the law. It is important not to misunderstand God's call to obedience as a new version of the covenant of works, whereby the people must render perfect obedience to God's commands in order to receive the blessings of the covenant. The Mosaic covenant falls under the covenant of grace. The sacrificial system included in the law attests to the fact that this covenant is one of grace that makes provisions for the sins of God's people. The Israelites under the Mosaic covenant do not earn salvation by works, but by grace. Their obedience is not a precondition for God's redemption, but a response to it. Before God gives the law, He calls Moses to remember how God kept His covenant with Abraham by delivering his offspring from Egypt. The next words God says are, "Now therefore" (Exodus 19:5). Because of the covenant that God has established and is continuing through the Israelites and because of the grace He has already given, now therefore obey; now therefore keep the commands of the covenant. This principle applies to all who are under the covenant of grace. We do not obey in order to earn salvation; we obey because we have been saved. God must first set us apart as holy before obedience is possible, and in fact, the Israelites had to be ceremonially purified before they received the law. We can do no good thing on our own, but when we are justified by faith in Jesus Christ, the result is obedience. Salvation does not leave us unchanged, but we are sanctified as we grow in the righteousness that has already been credited to us. Good works are evidence of faith, and God is calling the Israelites to live out of their redemption as they walk in holiness.

The result of this covenant is that the Israelites will be God's treasured possession, which Deuteronomy 7 affirms is a people chosen by His grace through His covenant, a kingdom of priests and a holy nation. It is to this end that God gives the Israelites the law, which includes the Ten Commandments as well as many additional laws. This covenant advances and expands the Abrahamic covenant in relation to its three major promises: the promise of a people, a land, and blessing.

The Mosaic covenant is a massive step in the direction of God fulfilling His promise to Abraham to make him the father of many nations, as his name denotes. The fulfillment of this promise to Abraham began with a family as Abraham fathered Isaac who fathered Jacob whose twelve sons multiplied exponentially in the land of Egypt. Now as God calls them out of Egypt, He establishes them not only as a family, but as a nation. They will be a holy nation, set apart as God's people and distinguished by the way they live in accordance with God's law. God began with a man that grew to a family and is now established as a nation, heading toward its final fulfillment as the global church, where people from every nation will be brought together under the promise.

God is also advancing His promise to give His people a land to dwell in. God has brought the Israelites out of slavery and will soon deliver them into the promised land of Canaan. The fifth commandment explicitly mentions the land that God will bring them into, exhorting them to live according to the law because its result will be long life in the land He will give them. God's creative order is one in which the world flourishes, and God calls the Israelites to live according to His ways.

Through God's covenant at Sinai, He provides a way for His people to be a blessing to all the nations, just as He promised Abraham. God says that by following the commands of the law, the Israelites would be a kingdom of priests. A priest functions as an intermediary between God and man, and in following the law, the Israelites would be serving this function for the other nations of the world. The law reflects God's holiness, and by walking in God's commands, God's people display His character to a world separated from Him. At the beginning of Jesus' commentary in the Sermon on the Mount, He exhorts his disciples to let their good works shine like lights so that those who see them may glorify God (Matthew 5:14-16). As the people of God display the holiness of God, it draws others to glorify God, and it is there that they find blessing beyond measure. It is there that they find the covenant of grace. It is there that they find redemption. God's people are a blessing to the world by showing them who God is as His image bearers, and the law reveals what it means to be an image bearer.

The covenant at Sinai is confirmed with a ceremony in Exodus 24. Moses reads the words that God has spoken, the Book of the Covenant, and the Israelites commit as a unified people to obey the covenant. The scene that unfolds is striking, as the Israelites make sacrifices of peace offerings and Moses sprinkles the blood of the sacrifice on the people. Remarkably, the people's oath to obey the voice of God is not accompanied by a ceremony in which the Israelite's assume the curse of the covenant upon themselves by walking through divided animals, but their oath is accompanied by a ceremony in which the blood of the peace offering symbolizes the atonement God provides for their inevitable sin. Even in commanding obedience, God makes a way for His people to be reconciled to Him despite their disobedience. Their peace with God comes not from their obedience, but from the blood of a sacrifice to atone for their disobedience, and it is because of the peace they have with God that they are empowered and compelled to obey His voice.

The Mosaic covenant is gracious. In it the law reveals God's holy character, our own sin as we fall short of the law's demands and the need for the better sacrifice, who is Christ, and how we are called to walk on obedience as God's people, holy and set apart not because of our own goodness, but because He chose us and set His love upon us.

How does the Mosaic covenant expand and advance the Abrahamic covenant as part of the overarching covenant of grace?

....

....

....

....

....

What does the dramatic scene of God speaking from the mountain reveal about His character?

....

....

....

....

Sometimes we can turn up our noses at the thought of the law and all the rules to follow. How does the idea of the law being a means for God's people to be a kingdom of priests to bless the nations affect your perspective of the law?

....

....

....

....

Christ Fulfills the Mosaic Covenant

Read Matthew 5:13-20, 1 Peter 1:1-2:12, Hebrews 10:1-14

> *Jesus perfectly displays and embodies the image of God through His perfect obedience.*

Jesus is the perfect fulfillment of the Mosaic covenant because He is the perfect fulfillment of the law. Christ did what we could never do — He lived a life of perfect obedience to the law of God. He lived a life of perfect righteousness.

The covenant of grace does not eliminate the standard of holiness to obtain God's covenant blessings. Rather, it provides a means for that standard to be met apart from ourselves. The covenant of grace does not declare that we do not need righteousness, but rather it invites us to receive the righteousness of Christ. The covenant of grace and all of its administrations require perfect obedience — something that we could never provide — and that obedience is found in Jesus Christ. That is why Jesus can say in Matthew 5 that we can only enter the kingdom of heaven if we have a righteousness that is far greater than the scribes and the Pharisees. Perfect righteousness is required, Christ has fulfilled it on our behalf, and His righteousness is credited to us when we put our faith in Him. The law does not pass away and the need for obedience is not eliminated, but Christ fulfills it in our place.

In Matthew 5, Jesus is firm in his admonition not to treat the law as if it has been abolished. We should not think that because we have been given grace we can ignore the demands of the law. In the Mosaic covenant, God's means by which His people would be a blessing to the nation was through their adherence to the law. In following the law, they would be reflecting His holy image and drawing people to God as they glorify Him. Now in the Sermon on the Mount, Jesus calls us to do the same. We are to do good works in accordance with the perfect law of God so that others will see them and glorify God, whose image we display. Jesus perfectly displays and embodies the image of God through His perfect obedience. In fact, He is fully divine, which is why Paul can describe Him as the image of the invisible God in Colossians 1:15 and the exact imprint of God's nature in Hebrews. Jesus reflects the image of God by His perfect righteousness, credits that righteousness to us by faith, and empowers us to walk in obedience as we increasingly are transformed into that same image (2 Corinthians 3:18).

When God gave the law to Moses and the Israelites, they participated in a covenant ceremony in which they were sprinkled with the blood of the peace offering. 1 Peter begins with a reference to this ceremony, saying that we who believe are sprinkled with the blood of Jesus Christ. Jesus Himself uses identical language to describe His blood that is to be shed as "my blood of the covenant," indicating His fulfillment of this ceremony for the forgiveness of sins (Matthew 26:28). Jesus is the fulfillment of the Mosaic Covenant not only because He follows the law perfectly, but also because He makes peace for us by bearing the covenant curse. He is the ultimate sacrifice who atones for our sin, the better sacrifice of which the sacrifices of bulls and oxen in the law given to Moses are merely shadows. The sacrifices required by the law had to be made year by year and were insufficient to cover sins, but they point to the once for all sacrifice of Christ through whom we are forgiven, purified, and have eternal peace with God.

The law demands that we be holy as God is holy (Leviticus 20:26), and the requirements of the law reveal what it means to reflect God's holy character. This type of obedience is only possible because of the sacrifice of Christ. We are sinful beyond measure, and we can only obey as a result of the purifying work of Christ on our behalf. Peter reiterates the command to imitate God's holiness, calling us to walk in obedience because of what Christ has done on our behalf. Christ is the One who causes us to receive the blessings of the covenant of grace, to receive an inheritance that is imperishable, undefiled, and unfading. We are saved not by following the law but by faith in the One who followed it perfectly, and our response to that salvation should be a life that flows out of that new identity of righteousness in Christ. Our salvation is not free, but it was bought with the costliest payment, the precious blood of Christ, not so that we could go on sinning, but so that we would be made holy. Christ fulfilled the demands of the law and bore the punishment for our sins so that we could bear His image.

When God announced the Mosaic covenant in Exodus 19, He said that the people of Israel would be His treasured possession, a holy nation, and a kingdom of priests. 1 Peter 2 repeats this same language, illustrating that Christ is the One who makes these things possible. It is through the blood of Christ that we have peace with God, that we are brought from enemies to sons, from "not a people" to "God's people." Jesus Christ is the One who declares us to be holy on account of His merit and it is His Spirit that transforms us into that holy image. It is Christ who empowers us to reflect God's image as a kingdom of priests to bless a watching world. Peter makes clear that we become a blessing to the nations through obedience to the law when he says that we become a kingdom of priests so that we may proclaim the excellencies of God who called us out of darkness into marvelous light. God has made us into a people—His people—and He has done it through His Son. He has done it through the blood of Christ. God has done it.

Christ did what we could never do—He lived a life of perfect obedience to the law of God.

How does the Mosaic covenant point forward to Jesus Christ?

....
....
....
....
....
....

*We tend to either try to earn our salvation by good works or to reject the rules
because we are under grace. How does understanding Christ's fulfillment
of the law on your behalf change the way you respond to it?*

....
....
....
....
....
....

*How have you fallen short of God's holy law this week? How does recognizing
your own need cause you to rejoice in the work of Christ?*

....
....
....
....
....
....

— WEEK 4 —

The Lord will fight for you, and you must be quiet.

Exodus 14:14

— DAY 6 —

Week Four *Reflection*

How did the text increase your understanding of covenants?

What did you observe about God's character?

What did you learn about the condition of mankind and about yourself?

How does the text point to the gospel?

How should you respond to this week's text? What is the practical application?

What specific action steps can you take this week to apply the text?

Delivered into the Promised Land

Read Joshua 1, Joshua 3, Joshua 4:19-24

God was with Joshua, just as He was with Moses, and He is with us as well.

God would certainly fulfill His covenant promises to bring Israel into the promised land, but perhaps not in the timing that they hoped. No sooner does Moses go up on Mt. Sinai after the Israelites agreed to follow the terms of the covenant God gave them than they break it, crafting a calf out of gold and worshiping the idol they make. God delays their entrance into the promised land and the Israelites wander in the desert for 40 years. Despite their disobedience, God's hand is still at work to fulfill His covenants. All throughout their wanderings, God provides the Israelites with food from heaven—manna and quail—to sustain the great nation that God promised and has now established. He calls Moses to build a tabernacle, a portable place of worship where God's presence would reside, which would contain the Ark of the Covenant, an even more particular representation of God's presence. The presence of God that Adam and Eve enjoyed and then lost at the fall, God is working to restore as He makes a way to dwell among His people. God reveals to Moses that although he will see the promised land with his own eyes, he will not enter it, only the generation after him will. God's timing may make it difficult to trust in God's promises, but even in the waiting God is always faithful.

The book of Joshua opens with the death of Moses and God's commissioning of Joshua to lead the Israelites into the promised land as a kind of new Moses. God is continuing to carry out His covenant promises throughout generations just as He has in the past. The promises of God were carried on throughout all of human history through the representatives of Adam, Noah, Abraham, Isaac, Jacob, Moses, and now Joshua. God promises to give Joshua and the people whom he represents the promised land with this assurance: "Just as I promised Moses" (Joshua 1:3). Joshua can be confident that his people will inherit the land because God is always faithful to His covenants, and God has made a covenant to give it to them. God's promises are always sure because He is a promise keeping God.

As God commissions Joshua to usher in this element of God's covenant promises, He commands him over and over to be strong and courageous. This exhortation is not founded in Joshua's self-possessed strength or courage, nor is it based on Joshua's own ability to lead the people into Canaan or defend them against their enemies. God's call to Joshua to be strong and courageous is based on the fact that God is with him.

Joshua does indeed cross the Jordan River and bring the Israelites into the promised land of Canaan. As the priests carrying the Ark of the Covenant step into the Jordan, which at this point is flooded to the point of overflowing, the waters flowing downstream are cut off and the Israelites walk through on dry ground. About 40,000 people pass through, all while the priests holding the Ark of the Covenant stand in the middle of the river. Just as God parted the Red Sea for Moses, so He parts the Jordan for Joshua, carrying on His promises to His people, promises to which He is always faithful. As the Israelites set up twelve stones as a memorial of the work of God on their behalf, they do it so that all who look upon them may know that God is mighty and fear Him. Looking back on how God brought the Israelites into Canaan is a poignant reminder of His mighty hand. Even when the promises of God seem impossible, He is mighty. The great I AM has shown himself time and time again to be able and faithful to fulfill every promise.

God was with Joshua, just as He was with Moses, and He is with us as well. Just like Joshua, we can look back on God's faithfulness to His people and His promises and trust that He will be faithful again. Just like Joshua, we can be sure that nothing can come against us and no enemy can defeat us because God is on our side. When God enters into covenant with His people, He obligates Himself to them, defending them and protecting them, fighting for them and concerning Himself with them. Just like Joshua, we can be courageous because we know that God will never abandon us, because God never abandons His covenant people. Just like Joshua, we can find courage in the ever-present help of the almighty, sovereign God of the universe who abounds in steadfast love for His people. If He is for us, there is absolutely nothing that can come against us. As we find ourselves in situations that seem as impossible to overcome as the overflowing Jordan River and as we see no way out of the trouble we find ourselves in like the Israelites with their heels backed up to the Red Sea, we can trust the God who does wonders. We can trust the God who is faithful to His covenants.

God calls Joshua to be strong and courageous because God is with Him. What does today's reading reveal about who God is, and how can those aspects of His character give you courage in your own situation?

....
....
....
....
....

List some similarities between Joshua and Moses based on today's reading. How does Joshua's portrayal as a new Moses illustrate God's faithfulness to His covenants?

....
....
....
....
....
....
....

What promises of God do you struggle to believe? How does the crossing of the Jordan encourage you in your doubt?

....
....
....
....
....

Week 5 - Day 2

—

God's Covenant
with David

Read 2 Samuel 7

The Israelites entered the land that God promised to Moses, but they quickly fell into sinful patterns and rejected the God who had been faithful to them. The very next generation of Israelites after those who crossed the Jordan did not know God or the covenant-keeping work He had done for their fathers (Judges 2:10). The book of Judges records a cycle of Israel's disobedience, God's judgment, and God's rescue. Time and time again the Israelites did what was right in their own eyes instead of what God commanded, and God sent judgment from other nations. As the Israelites found themselves desperate and in need of help, they repented and returned to God who repeatedly sent judges to deliver them from their enemies. The Israelites, like all sinful humans, were forgetful people, failing to remember God's faithfulness and blessings, and they repeatedly fell back into sin, starting the cycle afresh. As the narrative moves into the book of 1 Samuel, the Israelites demand a king, wishing to be like the sinful nations around them rather than ruled by God as a people set apart from the world. Saul becomes their king, and although his reign begins positively, it does not take long for Saul's pride to lead to destructive rebellion against God's commands rather than humble submission. God has the prophet Samuel anoint David, a shepherd, to be the next king over Israel in place of Saul. Saul pursues David, seeking to eliminate the threat to his throne, but God protects David and he is ultimately crowned king of Israel when Saul dies.

In 2 Samuel 7, God makes a covenant with David, another administration of the covenant of grace that would expand upon the covenants that came before it. David has been established as king over Israel, and while he now lives in a magnificent palace, the Ark of the Covenant is still housed in the tabernacle, which is literally a tent. David is called a man after God's own heart (1 Samuel 13:14), hungry for God's glory and presence, and David laments the fact his own dwelling place was more magnificent than the dwelling place of God and desires to build a house, a temple, for the presence of God to reside. However, God speaks to the prophet, Nathan, with a message for David. While David wants to build God a house, God says that He will build a house for David. In the words God gives to David through Nathan, He establishes a crucial covenant with David that gives further revelation of God's plan for His covenant of grace. As the covenants unfold, we see more and more of God's heart, His character, and His plan for His people.

God begins by reminding David of what God has done. Ever since God established His covenant with Moses, He has dwelt in a tent. This God who is Lord of all the universe has identified with His people, drawing near to them and living in tents just as they lived in tents. This God dwells with His people, and this God will continue to increasingly make

His dwelling place with them. God has chosen David to be his anointed king over Israel, calling him out of the sheep's pasture and into the king's palace to shepherd God's people, and He has continually protected David from His enemies. God reminds David of His faithfulness, and it is on the grounds of His own character that He makes promises of incredible blessings to David.

First, God promises to make David a great name. In making this promise, God continues and expands the promise He made to Abraham in Genesis 12:2. In addition to the promise of a great name, God restates the promise He made to Abraham of a land for his offspring—a promise that was carried on and confirmed through God's covenant with Moses and Joshua leading the people into the land of Canaan—this time promising David peace and rest from his enemies in the Israelites' own land under the rule of the Davidic king.

God also promises to build David a house. The Hebrew word translated as house here can have three different meanings: a palace, a temple, or a dynasty. This play on words in the text shows that while David wants to build a temple for God to dwell in, God intends to make David into a dynasty. God promises David that he and his offspring after him will be king over the people Israel, a promise anticipated in the Abrahamic covenant when God said kings would come from Abraham (Genesis 17:6). It is under the rule of the Davidic king, the anointed one, that God's people will live in righteousness as a blessing to the nations.

God makes many promises about David's seed, promises that will find partial fulfillment in the Old Testament, but ultimately find their fulfillment in Christ, just like the promises of the seed of Adam and Abraham. David's offspring will build God the house that David longs to build, a promise that finds partial fulfillment in the building of the temple by David's son and heir to his throne, Solomon. David's heir will also have a remarkable relationship to God: God will be his father, and he will be God's son. This language may seem commonplace to those who live after the cross, but the concept of a single person being called a son of God was unheard of when Israel as a whole was called God's son. God says that David's heir may experience punishment for sins, but he will not be cast off. God will not remove His steadfast love from him. The promises of God are sure, and not even sin will get in the way of God fulfilling every one. David's son, Solomon, would certainly make his fair share of mistakes, but Solomon's disobedience would not mean the end of God's covenant with David. God would still be faithful.

Perhaps the most incredible promise of the Davidic covenant is that David's house, his dynasty, his kingdom and throne, will never come to an end. The promise of the Davidic covenant is the promise of a king who will come from David's line and rule forever over God's people in a land that they will call home, a land where they will find peace and rest from everything that comes against them. The Davidic covenant is a sweet balm to the aching souls of people living in a sin cursed world. The Davidic covenant is a sure hope for God's people.

How does the Davidic covenant expand upon the covenants that came before it? What new information does it reveal about God's plan of redemption?

....
....
....
....
....
....

God's promises to His people under the covenant of grace are guaranteed even when we make mistakes. How does this knowledge change the way you view your own sin?

....
....
....
....
....
....

How does the brokenness of this world cause you to long for the kind of kingdom promised to David?

....
....
....
....
....
....

Christ Fulfills the Davidic Covenant

Read Isaiah 9:6-7, Matthew 1, Luke 1:26-33, Philippians 2:1-11

Even when we can't see God working, He is always faithful.

As the covenants unfold, each one progressively reveals more and more of God's plan of redemption through the overarching covenant of grace, each time pointing to Jesus Christ with greater clarity. The Davidic covenant gives the clearest picture so far of the promised Messiah to come. The word messiah means anointed one, and while David was God's anointed to rule as king over Israel, he is only a type—a shadow—pointing to the true and better king to come.

The Gospel of Matthew is saturated with kingdom language, and everything that Matthew includes in this book, from the language he chooses to the frequent Old Testament references, is working toward the goal of showing Christ as the promised Messiah King, the son of David who would be the Son of God ruling over God's people forever. It is no surprise then, that the Gospel of Matthew, which is also the first book in the New Testament, begins with the genealogy of Jesus that specifically highlights Jesus as the son of Abraham and of David. The Gospel of Luke follows suit, explicitly stating that Jesus Christ will be the Son of the Most High and will rule on the throne of His father, David, in a kingdom and rule that will never end. The long-awaited Messiah, the promised offspring of David, the long hoped for King is here, and His name is Jesus.

God's promise to David to give him a great name, the same promise he made to Abraham, finds its fulfillment in Christ. David's offspring not only has a great name, but the name that is above every name—a name so great that every knee will bow before Him and every tongue will confess His lordship. The name of Jesus will not only be known to Israel, but throughout all the world. This name will go on forever, because Jesus Christ will rule forever. He is the answer to the eternal kingdom promised to David. He is the One who will sit on the throne forever and ever (Hebrews 1:8). His government will never end, but will be everlasting (Isaiah 9:6-7).

In Jesus, the promise of a land of peace for the people of God where God dwells with them finds its fulfillment. Jesus Christ is Immanuel, God with Us. He is the Son of God, the second person of the Trinity, made man. In Christ's incarnation, God dwells among us (John 1:14). Even now, we live in a world that is broken by sin, not a land marked by never-ending peace and rest, but we look forward to the day when Christ will make it so. He will usher in the new heaven and the new earth, the place where God will dwell with us, the place where no evil can ever enter, the land of perfect peace ruled by the Prince of Peace who is the everlasting King. In the meantime, we live in the tension of the already but not yet. All around us may be chaos and confusion, but Christ Himself is our peace who has already brought us near to God (Ephesians 2:13-14). He leaves us His peace in the midst of a troubled world (John 14:27). Jesus calls out to us that we may come to Him and find rest from our burdens (Matthew 10:28). Even as we wait for the never-ending rest and peace when we will be home with God, we experience the rest and peace of Christ in the waiting.

Jesus is the embodiment of all the things that David, Solomon, and his descendants after could never perfectly fulfill. While Solomon built God a house in the temple, Christ would usher in a kingdom that would remain long after the temple lay in ruins. Jesus is not only a son of God, but is His only begotten Son, eternally in relationship with the Father. Jesus Christ bears the punishment for the sins of God's people, the true children of Abraham and David, so that God's steadfast love will not depart from them. David pointed forward to Christ, to the Messiah, but he was not Him. Jesus is the true and better Anointed One. He is the true and better King.

As the Old Testament story progresses, the promise of an unending Davidic kingdom seems to be lost. When Jerusalem was captured and the temple destroyed in 586 B.C., the line of Davidic kings was interrupted. It may have seemed as if God's promises were falling apart, but God always fulfills His promises. Nearly 600 years later, Jesus Christ, the Son of God and the son of David was born. Even when we can't see God working, He is always faithful. God does not work in our timing, but the waiting never negates God's promises. He will answer right on time. This King, announced by angels and worshiped by wise men, would not be conquered by any powers. This King conquered death and rose in victory to reign as King over all eternally as the eternal God. The promises of the Davidic covenant are not found in an endless line of human kings who rise to power and die, but in the one eternal King who raises us eternally with Him. In Christ, the kingdom is everlasting, the King is eternal, and the people of the kingdom have life unending.

Mark or note all references to the Davidic covenant in today's readings
(Include references to things like David, a kingdom, the son of God, etc.).
How does your understanding of the Davidic covenant change the way
you read these New Testament passages?

....

....

....

....

....

....

How do we experience the promises of the Davidic covenant in Christ now?
In what ways are we still waiting on them?

....

....

....

....

....

God's people waited through pain and hardship for the promised Messiah,
and many times it seemed as if God was not working to fulfill His promises.
In what ways are you waiting on the Lord right now, and how does the
birth of Jesus give you hope in the waiting?

....

....

....

....

....

....

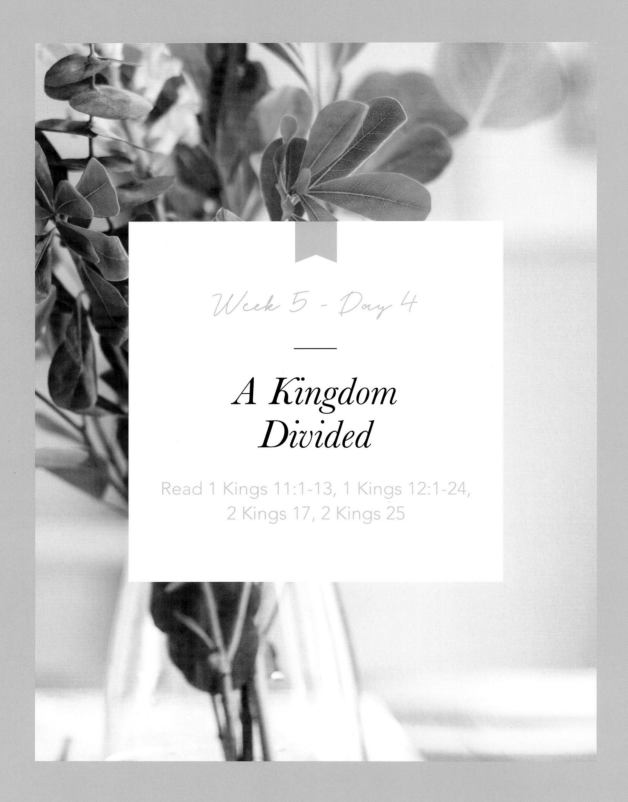

Week 5 - Day 4

—

A Kingdom Divided

Read 1 Kings 11:1-13, 1 Kings 12:1-24, 2 Kings 17, 2 Kings 25

In the waiting, God is faithful.
In the impossible, God is faithful.

God promises a messianic king who would rule over Israel in peace, but quickly the hope of a messianic king seems dim. The book of Kings shows the line of kings that come from David—the line that is to produce the Messiah—and as one king dies and the next rises to take his place, none of them are able to measure up to the promises God made to David. God's people are waiting on the promise of the righteous king, but they are not seeing its fulfillment. Nevertheless, God would be faithful to fulfill His promises in His good timing.

When the book of 1 Kings opens, David is king in his old age, and his throne passes onto his son, Solomon. Solomon builds a temple for the Lord—a glorious picture of God dwelling with His people—and brings partial fulfillment to the promise God made to David that his offspring would build God a house. However, it quickly becomes apparent that Solomon is not the Messiah that God's people have been waiting for. Solomon turns away from the commands of the Lord, breaking all of the requirements God gave for kings in Deuteronomy 17:14-20. He takes hundreds of wives for himself, including the daughters of other kings. He institutes worship of foreign gods in Israel and acquires excessive wealth for himself, using slave labor for his building projects. Solomon is not devoted to the Lord, but breaks the covenant, and so God warns that He will bring judgment on Solomon. God would take the kingdom away from Solomon after his death, but he would not abandon His promise to David.

God is certainly true to his word to bring judgment for Solomon's sin as king. Rehoboam, Solomon's son who becomes the next king, is just as corrupt and rebellious as his father before him. When the people of Israel call for Rehoboam to lighten the heavy load that Solomon laid on his slave laborers, Rehoboam instead treats them more harshly than before. As a result of this injustice, the people of Israel rebel against the king and set Jeroboam as king over them, leaving behind only the tribe of Judah who remains under the rule of the Davidic king. Thus, Israel is divided into two kingdoms, the northern kingdom, which is called Israel and whose capital city becomes Samaria, and the southern kingdom, which is called Judah and whose capital city is Jerusalem and remains under the rule of Davidic kings. The book of Kings recounts the reign of kings in both the northern and southern kingdoms, highlighting twenty kings in each kingdom. In the northern kingdom of Israel, none of these twenty kings are deemed good kings, but instead break the covenant and worship other gods. In the southern kingdom of Judah, only eight out of the twenty kings are deemed good kings.

All throughout the reign of these kings in the divided kingdom, God raises up prophets to call the people to repentance. The resounding cry of these prophets, whose words are

recorded in various books, is to repent and return. They call the kings and the people to repent of their sinful ways, and to return to the commands of God's law given in the Mosaic covenant. These prophets admonish the people to repent of worshiping idols and false gods, and to return to worshiping the God of Israel. Time and time again, the people ignore the warnings of the prophets and continue in their rebellion.

God's people have transgressed the covenant, and God's judgment falls upon them. In 2 Kings 17, the Assyrian Empire invades the northern kingdom, captures the city of Samaria, and exiles the Israelites. The text makes it abundantly clear that this event is not a random occurrence, but the just judgment of God against the people of Israel for their sin against Him. They are exiled because of their idolatry and evil practices. All that happens to Israel God had warned would take place in Deuteronomy 28 if they broke the covenant God gave to Moses. Less than 200 years later, the southern kingdom faces the same fate. While there are some good kings who try to bring Israel back to God, Judah is too far gone, having been ruled by kings who brought idol worship into the temple, instituted child sacrifice, and turned against God's commands. The Babylonian empire invades Jerusalem, destroys the temple, and sends the people of Judah, along with the line of Davidic kings, into exile.

At this point in Israel's history, the future seems bleak. God promised His people a land of peace to dwell in, but they have been exiled from the promised land. God promised to dwell among His people, but the dwelling place of God, the temple, has been destroyed. God promised a king from David's line who would rule in righteousness, but the line of desperately wicked kings has come to what seems like a hopeless end. It looks as if God has rejected His people, forgotten His covenants, and forsaken His promises. Nearly 600 years would pass without a Davidic king on the throne before God would begin to fulfill His promises in the most unexpected ways, but God would be faithful. God is always faithful. In the waiting, God is faithful. In the impossible, God is faithful. In the pain, God is faithful. We can't always see how, but God will come through. God is faithful.

What do these passages tell you about the seriousness of sin in God's eyes?

....

....

....

....

....

....

The human kings proved time and time again to be corrupted by sin.
How does the imperfection of human kings point to the need for a better king?

....

....

....

....

....

....

Have you ever gone through a time when it was difficult to see how God
would fulfill his promises? How does God's faithfulness to keep His covenants
despite the sin of Israel encourage you?

....

....

....

....

....

....

Promises of a New Covenant

Read Jeremiah 31:31-40, Ezekiel 11:14-20, Ezekiel 37

Where there was judgment, God will bring mercy and forgiveness.

The Israelites have broken the covenant that God made with them through Moses, and God's judgment has fallen upon them. God's people are left wondering what will come of His promises of dwelling with God in a land of peace ruled by a righteous Davidic king when they are exiled, their temple destroyed, and their land ruled by foreign kings. In the midst of their brokenness, God makes a new promise to establish a new covenant.

The new covenant is prophesied several times in the Old Testament. This covenant is different than the old covenant, which is a term that Scripture uses to refer to God's covenant with Moses, yet it encompasses and fulfills all of the previous administrations of the covenant of grace, from Adam to David. None of the promises of God are lost, but all will be fulfilled to an even greater measure in the new covenant in Christ Jesus where the covenant of grace finds its fulfillment. Unlike the previous administrations of the covenant of grace, the new covenant does not make way for more covenants that will follow, but it will be an everlasting covenant. The prophecies concerning this covenant acknowledge that although the Israelites in exile now endure God's righteous judgment for their sin, there are days coming when God will bring about redemption. By the grace of God and His faithfulness to His covenants, it won't always be this way.

In the new covenant, God's promise for His people to dwell in the promised land under the rule of a messianic king from David's line will find its fulfillment. God promises to bring not only the people of Judah back to the promised land, but the people of Israel as well, uniting God's people who are now divided as they are ruled by the promised Davidic king. This covenant will be different from the Mosaic covenant, because while God gave the Israelites His law written on stone tablets, under the new covenant He will write His law on their hearts. In the new covenant, God gives new life where there was once death, reviving dry bones and covering them with flesh so that they live again. Hearts of stone that are bent against God, He will replace with a new heart of flesh guided by His Holy Spirit. Because of the new heart that God will give, His people will have the ability to follow the commandments that they have broken, empowered by the Spirit to walk in obedience. This new heart will also be one heart, a heart shared among all of God's people that unites them under His commands of holiness for their own benefit (Jeremiah 32:39, Ezekiel 11:19). This promise means that hearts plagued by wickedness and sin will desire all that is holy and righteous and good, and, by God's grace, will be sanctified and ultimately rid of sin. Not only that, but all of their sins will be forgiven. Where there was judgment, God will bring mercy and forgiveness.

The greatest promise of the covenant is not a land as a place for God's people to live, but the God with whom they will dwell. Throughout all of Scripture, God is working to restore His presence to His people, the intimate communion with God that was broken in the garden. The promise that echoes over and over again and is now stated so clearly in the new covenant prophecies is that God will make His dwelling with His people. The greatest promise that God makes to His people is His presence. Many theologians refer to this promise woven throughout the Bible as the Immanuel Principle. He will dwell with us. He will be our God, and we will be His people, holy and righteous at last. Moreover, the vision that God gives for dwelling with His people is not one simply of proximity, but of intimate relationship. The prophecies of the new covenant in Jeremiah 31 describe the relationship between God and His people as one in which His people know Him. The Hebrew word for know here is *yada*`, a word that denotes not simply a knowledge of facts, but a personal, relational knowledge of someone. The new covenant promises that God's people will not just know who God is, but they will be in communion with Him.

The promise of the new covenant is the promise of restoration above and beyond all that was lost. It is the promise of God's presence with His people. It is the promise of a home with God marked by peace and not destruction under the perfect Messiah King. It is the promise of hearts turned permanently to God and cleansed of all sin. It is the promise of new and everlasting life brought forth from the death brought on by sin's curse. It is the promise that every covenant blessing will be made a reality for the people of God despite their faithlessness, because through it all God is faithful. This covenant and its promises are sure. As surely as God causes the sun to rise and the seasons to change, He will be faithful to His covenants. We could measure the expanse of the universe before God would ever cast us off and forsake His promises. These promises are not just for those who are physical descendants of those who received the promises, but it is for all who by faith believe in the promises of God. This new covenant is for us, and we can rest assured that God will bring it to completion.

None of the promises of God are lost, but all will be fulfilled to an even greater measure in the new covenant in Christ Jesus where the covenant of grace finds its fulfillment.

How were the people of Israel like the bones in the valley? How were you like the bones in the valley? What hope does the new covenant give?

....

....

....

....

....

....

Read back through Ezekiel 37 and note any references to previous covenants. How will the new covenant fulfill all the previous covenants?

....

....

....

....

....

As far as the Israelites could tell, God did not seem to be working to fulfill His promises to them, but God spoke to them with promises of hope through His prophets. God has also spoken to us through the Bible. How can God's promises in His Word give you hope when you can't see God's hand working?

....

....

....

....

....

....

— WEEK 5 —

Haven't I commanded you: be strong and courageous? Do not be afraid or discouraged, for the Lord your God is with you wherever you go.

Joshua 1:9

— DAY 6 —

Week Five *Reflection*

Answer the following questions about this week's Scripture passages.

How did the text increase your understanding of covenants?

What did you observe about God's character?

What did you learn about the condition of mankind and about yourself?

How does the text point to the gospel?

....

....

....

....

....

....

How should you respond to this week's text? What is the practical application?

....

....

....

....

....

....

What specific action steps can you take this week to apply the text?

....

....

....

....

....

....

Christ Ushers in the New Covenant

Read Luke 22:14-23

Nearly 600 years after the line of Davidic kings came to an end, the destruction of the temple, and the exile of God's people from the promised land, the One who would usher in the promised new covenant arrived. Jesus Christ was born in Bethlehem as the promised Messiah King who would bring about the blessings of the covenant at last. We find ourselves now in Luke 22, where years later Jesus announces the inauguration of the long-awaited new covenant.

The time has come for the annual Passover celebration, and on this night, Jesus would celebrate the last Passover and institute the Lord's Supper in its place. The Passover is a feast day instituted by God in Exodus 12 to call the people to remember how God delivered them from the wrath of God's judgment and out of slavery in Egypt. On the night of the first Passover, God sent a plague that took the life of every firstborn in Egypt, but for the Israelites, His covenant people, He provided a way for death to pass over them. Every Israelite family was to take a spotless lamb, without any blemishes or imperfections, and paint its blood over their door post so that the angel of the Lord would pass over their houses and spare their lives. This animal represented a substitute that would take the wrath of God in their place, but a mere lamb would never be enough to remove the covenant curse from people who had violated God's covenant of works. The Passover points forward to a true and better sacrifice. The Passover points to Jesus.

As the disciples eat the familiar Passover meal of lamb and bitter herbs, Jesus does something new. He takes bread, breaks it, and tells them, "This is my body, which is given for you." He then takes wine and says, "This cup is the new covenant in my blood, which is poured out for you." By referring to His body and His blood, Jesus is making an important statement about the purpose of His impending death. When animals were prepared for sacrifice, they were divided into two parts: their bodies, a portion of which were given to the priest and the rest burned on the altar, and their blood, which was drained from the animal. Jesus uses this intentional language on this particular night as they feast within yards of the temple where animal sacrifices are offered to show that He Himself is a sacrifice given for His people, and not just any sacrifice, but the true Passover lamb. He is the One who is truly without blemish or spot. He is the One who lived a life of total holiness as the Son of God, unstained by sin.

Jesus' sacrifice of His own body and blood is substitutionary. Jesus indicates that His sacrifice is made on behalf of His covenant people as he says, "Is given for you." This language calls to mind the description of the suffering servant in Isaiah 53, whose wounds pay for our sins, and not his own. The remarkable statement that Jesus is making is that through His sacrifice He takes the penalty for our sins in our place. When Jesus takes the cup, He directly references the new covenant prophesied in Jeremiah 31, connecting His death to the inauguration of the new covenant blessings. The image of the cup carries great significance throughout Scripture as it represents the wrath of God against sin (Isaiah 51:17, Matthew 26:39), and the new covenant in Christ's blood is a picture of Christ absorbing the wrath of God for sin that was rightly due to us. Apart from Christ, we are all condemned under the covenant of works because every one of us are covenant-breakers. Jesus Christ, God incarnate, is the only human who has ever met the requirements of the covenant of works. In Jesus' death, He takes on our sin as His own and absorbs the curse of the covenant on our behalf so that we might obtain the covenant blessings that we never deserved. It is only by Christ's death that the promises of the new covenant are possible.

When Jesus sits down to have this meal with His disciples, He expresses that He has eagerly desired to eat this Passover meal with them. Even though Jesus knew what this meal represented, that the very next day He would experience pain beyond anything we could imagine, He longed to eat this meal with His disciples. Not only would Judas betray Him, but Peter would deny Him and every one of His twelve disciples would abandon Him in His time of suffering (Mark 14:50), yet He longs to celebrate with them. Here we see a picture of the incredible love of Christ for His people. We see the love of the Savior who knows the wickedness of our hearts and freely gives Himself up for us. We see a love that will pay the greatest price to dwell with those who have abandoned Him. We see the love of God who remains faithful even when we are faithless and who gives His very Son for us when we have turned our backs on Him. This love is an unbreakable covenant love.

How does the language and the imagery of Jesus' body and blood show him to be the true sacrifice that makes the new covenant possible?

....

....

....

....

....

....

Go back and read Jeremiah 31:31-40. What similarities do you see with that passage and today's reading?

....

....

....

....

....

....

What does today's passage reveal about the love of God?
How does it give you comfort and hope today?

....

....

....

....

....

....

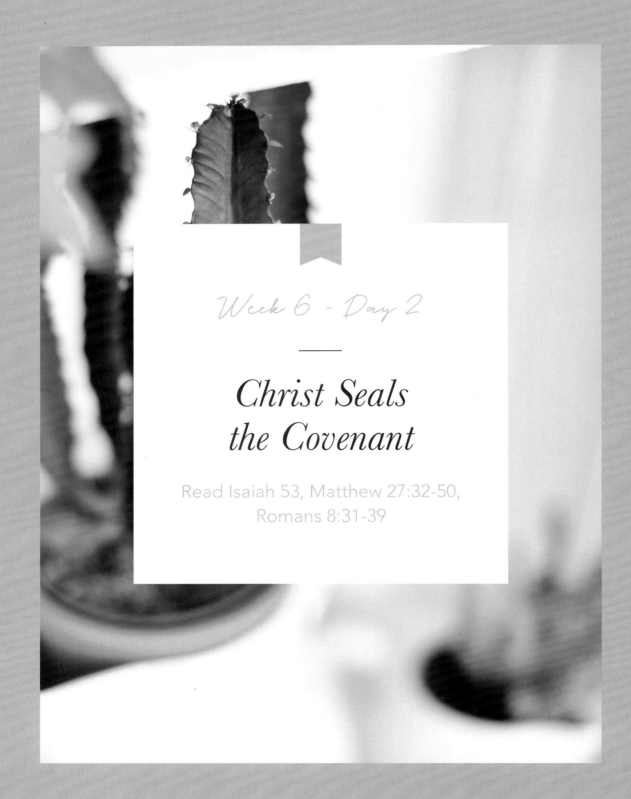

Christ Seals
the Covenant

Read Isaiah 53, Matthew 27:32-50,
Romans 8:31-39

We have been purchased by the blood of Christ as God's covenant people, and we can rest completely secure in His love.

Isaiah 53 prophecies about the suffering servant who would stand in the place of God's people. This promised One would pay the penalty of the covenant of works in our place and secure its blessings for us under the covenant of grace, which finds its culmination in the new covenant. This passage is perhaps the messianic prophecy with the clearest and most obvious connections to Jesus Christ. Isaiah 53 shows Jesus' death on the cross as the means by which God fulfills the promise of the new covenant to forgive the sins of His people. God is a holy and just God whose very character necessitates that He punish sin. Under the covenant of grace, God pours out His wrath not on His rebellious people, but on His sinless Son who pays their penalty in their place. This means by which Christ saves is known as substitutionary atonement. The blood of Christ, far greater than the blood of sacrifices under the old covenant, atones once for all the sins of God's people (Hebrews 10:10).

Every person is condemned under the curse of the covenant of works, but for those under the covenant of grace by faith in Jesus Christ, we go from cursed to blessed and from death to life. This act of grace is possible not because God simply withholds His judgment, for it would be unjust for God to let wickedness go unpunished, but because "Christ redeemed us from the curse of the law by becoming a curse for us, because it is written, 'Cursed is everyone who is hung on a tree'" (Galatians 3:13). As Christ hangs on the tree, nailed the cross, He is cursed on our behalf, absorbing the fullness of God's wrath for those who put their faith in Him. He takes on our sin as His own, even though He Himself is without sin, pays its penalty, and in its place credits His righteousness to us. Just as Abraham's faith in the promises of God to be fulfilled in Christ was counted to him as righteousness, so our faith is counted to us as righteousness through faith in Christ Jesus. He became our sin so we could become His righteousness (2 Corinthians 5:21). Jesus receives the penalty of the covenant of works so that we might receive its blessings under the covenant of grace.

We have been purchased by the blood of Christ as God's covenant people, and as His people, we can rest completely secure in His love. When God enters into a covenant with us, He obligates Himself to us. His very character requires that He remain faithful to His covenants. Christ sealed the new covenant in His blood, declaring, "It is finished!" as He gave up His own life for our sake (John 19:30) and He secured the blessings of the covenant for us as He rose from the dead in victory, proving His work on our behalf to be effective (1 Corinthians 15:21, 1 Timothy 3:16). We are His covenant people if we

have faith in Christ, and that means that God is for us. His love for us was great enough to give even His most precious, beloved Son so that we, sinners though we are, could be welcomed as His children. This God who paid the highest price to enter into covenant with us will not abandon us now. His love for us is unbreakable, and there is absolutely nothing that can separate us from that love. As His covenant people, we will never again have to experience the sting of separation that Adam and Eve felt as they were sent out of the garden. Through Christ, He is our God, and we are His people.

This promised one would pay the penalty of the covenant of works in our place and secure its blessings for us under the covenant of grace, which finds its culmination in the new covenant.

What similarities do you see between the suffering servant in Isaiah 53 and the crucifixion of Jesus?

....
....
....
....
....

Re-read Paul's list of things that cannot separate us from God in Romans 8:35-39.
What fears do you most identify with?
How does the reality of God's covenant love confront those fears?

....
....
....
....
....
....

God paid the highest price to make us His covenant people.
Write a prayer of thanksgiving in response to today's reading.

....
....
....
....
....
....

Christ Consummates the Covenant

Read Isaiah 60, Revelation 21

Christ inaugurates the new covenant at His crucifixion, but it will find its final fulfillment at the second coming of Christ when He will usher in the new heaven and new earth and bring about the consummation of the kingdom of God. Isaiah 60 is a prophetic passage that anticipates this new covenant picture of a restored Israel, and it is one of the many passages that John references in Revelation 21. Revelation looks forward to events that as of yet have remained unfulfilled in the form of visions that God gives to John, and chapter 21 provides a beautiful picture of the new covenant fulfilled in Christ, bringing with it all the blessings of the covenants that came before it.

Revelation 21 opens up with a vision of a new heaven and a new earth to replace the old heaven and earth that will have passed away. We as believers look forward to the day when Christ will return, taking what is broken and making it new. This is the fulfillment of the new covenant promise to return God's people to the promised land, a land that Christ reveals to be far better than the first Jerusalem from which the Israelites were exiled. This New Jerusalem is the new and better homeland that the people of faith in the Old Testament longed for. This new land is the city that God was preparing for them (Hebrews 11:16). This New Jerusalem is not like the first, but is dressed like a bride on her wedding day, a fulfillment of the promise that God made in Isaiah 60:9 to make Israel beautiful.

This chapter envisions the fulfillment of God's covenant with David and the promise that a king would come from his line and would reign eternally over God's people. A voice calls out from the throne, described in Revelation 7 as being occupied by the Lamb, who is Jesus Christ, the true Passover lamb. From the throne, Christ announces the fulfillment of the promise that God has been revealing since the fall—the dwelling place of God is with man at last. He will be their God, and they will be His people. The promises of the new covenant in Ezekiel 37:27 and Jeremiah 31:33—the promises that have been at the heart of every one of God's covenants under the covenant of grace—the promises are fulfilled in Christ. He declares Himself to be the Alpha and Omega—the first and last letters of the Hebrew alphabet—the beginning and the end. From before the foundations of the earth into eternity, He is the fulfillment of every covenant. From beginning to end, every promise finds its answer in Jesus.

The city of God in the new heaven and new earth is a city of peace. Where Israel experienced judgment and wrath, slavery and exile, suffering and brokenness, now all of God's people will dwell in a land without mourning and without weeping, without sickness and without death, without grief and suffering. God Himself will wipe away all of our tears because Christ has borne our sorrows. Christ has made a way for us to dwell in peace through the covenant of peace (Ezekiel 27:6) because He has made peace for us. He has reconciled us to God with His blood, and now we can dwell in His presence. It is done. God's judgment on sin is complete, the painful effects of sin are eradicated, and the promise of a land of peace given throughout the administrations of the covenant of grace is fulfilled.

As we move throughout Scripture, we see God's plan of redemption unfold, from creation, to fall, to redemption, and here at last we see God's restoration as His plan reaches its consummation. Jesus Christ restores all that was lost at the fall, declaring that He is making all things new. Jesus Christ offers water from the spring of life without payment because He has already paid for it, bringing dry bones to life. The image of God marred at the fall is restored as His people are glorified with Christ. Furthermore, God's people are called sons. God promised that David's offspring would be a son to God and God would be to him a Father, and now that same language is used to describe all those who conquer—those who are more than conquerors through Jesus Christ (Romans 8:37)—as His sons and daughters. We rejoice that the Son of God rules on David's throne eternally, and we rejoice that we too are adopted in love to be sons and daughters with Christ and co-heirs of His kingdom (Romans 8:17, Romans 8:29, John 17:23).

John sees a vision of the Bride of the Lamb. Where God describes the broken marriage covenant between God and Israel in Jeremiah 31, here that relationship is restored in this new covenant. John then has a closer look at the New Jerusalem coming down out of heaven. It has twelve gates with the names of the twelve tribes of Israel as well as twelve foundations with the names of the twelve apostles, showing that God has carried His promises to Abraham all the way through to His apostles and into eternity. The promises of God are not broken, but there is continuity between every covenant under the covenant of grace. In this city there is no temple, but instead God Himself, the Father and the Son, are the temple. Sin has been defeated, and there is no longer anything to separate us from God's presence, not even the walls of a temple. There is no sun, but the Lamb, Jesus Christ, is the lamp that gives light, just as God promised in Isaiah 60, along with the promise that the kings of the world will bring its glory into the city of God found in the same chapter that finds it fulfillment here. All that will enter will be good and glorious, and nothing evil will enter its gates. There is only peace here.

The promise of the New Jerusalem is not a promise exclusively reserved for ethnic Israel, but it is a promise for all those who by faith in Jesus Christ are children of God. They are the true sons of Abraham and children of the promise. The bride of Christ is the church, the body of believers, comprised of people from every tribe, tongue, and nation, brought together by the blood of Christ (Ephesians 5:25, Revelation 7:9). As part of God's covenant people, the hope of eternity is for us. May we rejoice in the hope of the glory of that day.

*Re-read Revelation 21 and note any place where you see
one of God's promises fulfilled.*

*How does the vision of the new heaven and new earth give you hope as
you live in a world that is still broken?*

*The description of the new heaven and new earth is one that should cause our hearts
to rejoice in hopeful expectation. Write a prayer of worship and thanksgiving in
response to the promises found in today's Scripture passages.*

Waiting on the Covenant

Read 1 Corinthians 13:12, John 1:1-18, Romans 7:15-25, 2 Corinthians 4:16-18

The reality of the new covenant is one in which Christ reigns as King over God's people who dwell with Him and know Him in a land of peace and righteousness that is unstained by sin. In many ways, the kingdom of God is already here, but in other ways, it has not yet arrived in its fullness. Christ has inaugurated the kingdom, but it has not yet been consummated. We will see the fullness of God's kingdom at Christ's second coming, but until then, we live in the tension of the already and the not yet, rejoicing in the finished work of Christ and longing for the day when our faith will be made sight.

One promise we experience in part but will one day experience in full is the presence of God. When Christ came to earth as a human being, the world experienced the presence of God in a very real way. Jesus Christ is Immanuel, God with us, and although no one except the Son has ever seen the Father, Jesus Christ revealed who the Father is because He is the image of the invisible God and the perfect imprint of His nature (Colossians 1:15, Hebrews 1:3). After Jesus' ascension, God sent the Holy Spirit to dwell within believers who are themselves built up together as the temple of God and His holy dwelling place (Ephesians 2:22, 1 Peter 2:5), and before He left He told His disciples that He would be with them always (Matthew 28:20). God is with us and we can experience His presence now, but we do not yet experience the fullness of His presence. In this present age between Christ's first and second comings, we see with blurry vision the things that will be made clear. We experience God's presence now, but when Christ brings in the new heaven and new earth, we will experience His manifest presence. We will see God face to face. We will know Him to a degree that we cannot now know Him.

The new covenant also promises new hearts for God's people with His law written on them. This promise is the hope of hopelessly diseased and wicked hearts now healed and purified, rid of the cancer of sin and made new in complete holiness. It is the promise of a heart that loves holiness and walks in obedience, untainted by sin. Through faith in the atoning work of Christ on the cross, we are declared to be righteous, justified and freed from the curse of sin. We become new creations (2 Corinthians 5:17), delighting in God's holy commands. God takes our heart of stone and gives us a heart of flesh, but like Paul we still battle against our sinful flesh. We are empowered by the indwelling Holy Spirit to put our sin to death, to turn away from sin, and to walk in obedience, but the sin in our hearts is not yet eradicated. One day we will be glorified and totally free from the presence of sin, but between our justification and glorification is the lifelong process of sanctification. We who are in Christ are being purified day by day, transformed into the image of Jesus Christ, being made more and more holy until the day when the new covenant is totally fulfilled and not only are our sins forgiven, but our sinning ceases.

The vision of the valley of dry bones in Ezekiel 37 looks forward to the new covenant promises of new resurrection life. For those who put their faith in Christ and are united to Him as their covenant head under the covenant of grace, we are united to Him in both His death, by which He pays the penalty of the covenant curse on our behalf, and in His resurrection (Romans 6:5). All who are in Christ have undergone a spiritual resurrection, being raised from our state of spiritual death in our sin to life in Christ (Ephesians 2:5), but we still await a physical resurrection. When Christ returns, our perishable bodies will be raised imperishable, no longer afflicted by death and pain, but glorious like the resurrected body of Christ (1 Corinthians 15:42, Philippians 3:21). In the meantime, our bodies still bear the curse of sin. They are marked by decay and are fading away. We experience the suffering of chronic illness and loved ones gone too soon.

As we await Christ's second coming, how can we live in this tension of the already and the not yet? We must keep our eyes fixed on eternity. Like Christ who endured the cross for the joy set before Him (Hebrews 12:12), we look to the hope of eternity, knowing that everything we experience now will result in glory. We actively turn away from sin and walk in obedience by the power of the Holy Spirit, knowing that none of it is in vain but matters for eternity (1 Corinthians 15:58). We seek to know Him daily, searching Him out in His Word and communing with Him in prayer. We mourn the effects of sin and the toll it takes on our bodies, lamenting the death brought on by the curse of the fall, but we do not grieve as those without hope (1 Thessalonians 4:13). We set our eyes, our minds, and our hearts on eternity. This world is not as it should be, but it won't always be this way. Christ will return and bring with Him the fullness of the blessings of the covenant of grace. Christ will make all things new. This hope is guaranteed because it has been promised by God in His covenant of grace, and God always keeps His covenants. Fix your eyes on the covenant-keeper.

We experience the promises of God in part, but not yet in full. What are some specific ways you have experienced God's promises in your own life that you can celebrate?

....

....

....

....

....

....

What painful or difficult circumstances are you facing now?
How does the future reality of Christ's second coming help you to grieve with hope?

....

....

....

....

....

....

As we taste and experience the goodness of the Lord, our hearts long for more of Him. How can you intentionally experience God's goodness this week?

....

....

....

....

....

....

Every Covenant Fulfilled in Christ

Read Hebrews 13:20-21

He is the perfect covenant-keeper and the hope for covenant-breakers.

From before the foundations of the world all the way to eternity, every covenant of God finds its fulfillment in Jesus Christ. He takes on the curse and He accomplishes the blessings. He is the perfect covenant-keeper and the hope for covenant-breakers. He is the yes to every promise from beginning to end (2 Corinthians 1:20).

Jesus Christ is the One who accomplishes our redemption in the covenant of redemption. Before time began, the Son covenanted with the Father and the Spirit to save a people for God's own possession. Knowing in full the wickedness of man that would result from the fall and the pain that He would endure as a result of their sin and rejection, in love He entered a binding agreement to take on human flesh as the man Jesus Christ, bear the penalty of sin's curse in His excruciating death, and be raised to new life, all so that we can experience the blessings of the covenant and all so that we could experience life with God to the glory of God. Since before the foundations of the world, Jesus has always been the plan.

Jesus is the promised seed of the woman who would defeat Satan. His heel was bruised in His death, but it is that same death that crushes the serpent's head. Death could not hold him (Acts 2:24), but Christ was raised in victory over death, over sin, and over the deceiver. Even in the most heinous and wicked act in human history, the crucifixion of the Son of God Himself, what the enemy meant for evil, God intended for good (Genesis 50:20). Jesus is the true and better Adam, bringing life through His obedience to the covenant of works where Adam's disobedience brought death. Christ kept the covenant that we broke. He not only fulfilled its requirements, but He took on its curse and secured its blessings on our behalf.

Christ is the One who preserves God's people as Noah and his family were preserved in the ark. The only thing separating us from eternal damnation is the grace of God manifested in the life, death, and resurrection of Jesus Christ. Christ will usher in the final judgment to which the flood points, and Christ is the One who offers a way through judgment. He is the One who will restore the creation that God promised to spare in His covenant with Noah, making all things new when He comes again.

Jesus Christ fulfills the promise that God gave to Abraham and to Moses and David to bring God's people into a land of peace. He ushers in the new and true promised land, the new heaven and new earth, where all of God's people will dwell in safety. He makes a way for us to be reconciled to God so that we can live in peace with Him rather than separation from Him as His enemies. He is the great name promised to Abraham as the name that is above every name (Philippians 2:9). In Christ, Abraham receives the promise of offspring as numerous as the stars. Jesus' work on the cross raises up sons for Abraham beyond his physical descendants to include people from every tribe, tongue, and nation who are sons of Abraham and sons of God by faith in the Messiah. In this way, Christ brings blessing to every nation as Abraham's promised seed. He provides the ultimate blessing, the blessing of salvation that brings us to God.

Jesus is the only One who perfectly fulfills the law given to Moses. In our union with Him as our covenant head under the covenant of grace, righteousness by works that He earned is credited to us by grace through faith. It is through His power that we can increasingly walk in obedience to the holy requirements of the law, and it is through His work that we will follow it in perfect holiness when He returns. It is He who empowers us to be a kingdom of priests, reflecting the image of God that He is restoring in us to bring others to Him.

Christ is the true Messiah King from David's line. He is the One who ushered in the kingdom and who now reigns at the right hand of the Father and in our hearts as Lord of our lives (Hebrews 8:1, Colossians 3:15), and it is He who will consummate the kingdom at His second coming when He will be seated on the throne in our midst. He is the true temple of God as Immanuel, God with us, and His return will bring about the dwelling place of God with us without the need for a temple.

Jesus Christ inaugurates, seals, and consummates the new covenant. Where there is death, He brings life. Where there is sin, He accomplishes righteousness. Where there is brokenness, He makes all things new. When we look to Christ, we can see the faithfulness of God to fulfill every promise. God has been, is, and will always be a covenant-keeper, and He fulfills every covenant in Christ.

How does seeing Christ as the fulfillment of every promise of God change the way you view Scripture as a whole?

....
....
....
....
....
....

How has your study of covenants increased your understanding of the hope that Christ brings?

....
....
....
....
....
....

According to Hebrews 13:20-21, what impact do the covenants have on our everyday lives?

....
....
....
....
....
....

— WEEK 6 —

nor height nor depth, nor any other created thing will be able to separate us from the love of God that is in Christ Jesus our Lord.

Romans 8:39

— DAY 6 —

Week Six *Reflection*

Answer the following questions about this week's Scripture passages.

How did the text increase your understanding of covenants?

What did you observe about God's character?

What did you learn about the condition of mankind and about yourself?

How does the text point to the gospel?

....
....
....
....
....
....

How should you respond to this week's text? What is the practical application?

....
....
....
....
....
....

What specific action steps can you take this week to apply the text?

....
....
....
....
....
....

What is the Gospel?

THANK YOU FOR READING AND ENJOYING THIS STUDY WITH US!

We are abundantly grateful for the Word of God, the instruction we glean from it, and the ever-growing understanding about God's character from it. We're also thankful that Scripture continually points to one thing in innumerable ways: the gospel.

We remember our brokenness when we read about the fall of Adam and Eve in the garden of Eden (Genesis 3), when sin entered into a perfect world and maimed it. We remember the necessity that something innocent must die to pay for our sin when we read about the atoning sacrifices in the Old Testament. We read that we have all sinned and fallen short of the glory of God (Romans 3:23), and that the penalty for our brokenness, the wages of our sin, is death (Romans 6:23). We all are in need of grace, mercy, and most importantly: we all need a Savior.

We consider the goodness of God when we realize that He did not plan to leave us in this dire state. We see His promise to buy us back from the clutches of sin and death in Genesis 3:15. And we see that promise accomplished with Jesus Christ on the cross. Jesus Christ knew no sin yet became sin so that we might become righteous through His sacrifice (2 Corinthians 5:21). Jesus was tempted in every way that we are and lived sinlessly. He was reviled, yet still yielded Himself for our sake, that we may have life abundant in Him. Jesus lived the perfect life that we could not live, and died the death that we deserved.

The gospel is profound yet simple. There are many mysteries in it that we can never exhaust this side of heaven, but there is still overwhelming weight to its implications in this life. The gospel is the telling of our sinfulness and God's goodness, and this gracious gift compels a response. We are saved by grace through faith, which means that we rest with faith in the grace that Jesus Christ displayed on the cross (Ephesians 2:9). We cannot save ourselves from our brokenness or do any amount of good works to merit God's favor, but we can have faith that what Jesus accomplished in His death, burial, and resurrection was more than enough for our salvation and our eternal delight. When we accept God, we are commanded to die to our self and our sinful desires, and live a life worthy of the calling we've received (Ephesians 4:1). The gospel compels us to be sanctified, and in so doing, we are conformed to the likeness of Christ Himself.

This is hope. This is redemption.
This is the gospel.

Thank You

FOR STUDYING GOD'S
WORD WITH US!

CONNECT WITH US:

@THEDAILYGRACECO
@KRISTINSCHMUCKER

CONTACT US:

INFO@THEDAILYGRACECO.COM

SHARE:

#THEDAILYGRACECO
#LAMPANDLIGHT

WEBSITE:

WWW.THEDAILYGRACECO.COM